ADOPTION 101:
The Basics To Begin Your Adoption Journey

Stacy Gleaton, LCSW

Edited by: Marion Archer with Making Manuscripts

Cover Design by: Jena Brignola

Formatting by: Rebecca Manuel with Bibliophile Productions

Printed in the United States of America

First Printing, August 2022

ISBN:

979-8-88757-503-2 Print

979-8-88757-504-9 Digital

INTRODUCTION

My goal in this publication is for you to gain the understanding, comfort, and competence to take the first step in your adoption journey. This book is not designed to be a complete guide as there are many varied paths that adoption can take. However, this book will give you the foundation and direction to start.

The photos printed in this book are used with the permission of the prospective adoptive parents and adoptive parents.

To those families, thank you for allowing me to share photos from your adoption journey.
Chris and Julie Barnes
Jade and Jeanette Barnett
Dave and Mandy B.
Brenner and Stephanie Campbell
Todd and Lisa E.
Zack and Meagan Eastburn
BJ and Jeana Ford
Casey and Lacy Jones

Eric and Kristy Muller
Jeffrey and Teryn Neuer
Bradley and Brittany Noack
Eric and Rebekah Peele
Radames and Tiffany Perez
Justin and Selena Savell
Weston and Jessica Tramell
Chad and Janna Usher
Edward and Karen Williams
Nathan and Lisa Yocom

A special thanks to my friends who helped me polish this document into a book.
Ami Allen
Marion Archer
Jena Brignola
Daniel Gleaton
Janet Hitchcock
Chelle Northcutt
Becca Manuel

prospective adoptive "big brothers" pose with
their future younger sister

CHAPTER ONE
OVERVIEW OF THE ADOPTION PROCESS AND HOW TO GET STARTED

Adoption is the act of becoming legally responsible for a child, as if that child was your biological child. There are inherent rights and responsibilities of being legally responsible for a child. For example, you decide if your child will attend a public or private school, you decide the medical care your child will or will not receive, and you financially support your child.

The simple version of the adoption process is as follows. In order for a child to be adopted, that child has to be "legally freed," meaning that the legal responsibilities of their biological parents have to be ended in order for another adult (or adults) to be able to assume that legal responsibility. The prospective adoptive parents are required to complete and pass a home study. The adoptee is placed in their home. Then, the adoption is finalized in court. There are many contingencies involved to ensure each step is completed correctly.

Before you start your adoption journey, you will need to decide what type of adoption would best fit you. You can adopt a child from foster care through your state's Child Protective Services department or you can adopt a child through a private adoption (a child that is not in foster care). If you decide that a private adoption fits you the best, you can then choose to adopt domestically or internationally. If you select a domestic adoption, then you have the freedom to go through an adoption agency or not. We will explore each of these options in the following chapters.

---

*Please note that each state is governed by its own statutes, which can vary state to state; however, they generally follow the same process. You can search online for your state's adoption statutes or ask your local CPS office how to find them. Also, each adoption agency will vary in their costs, services offered, and matching processes.

Each adoption is different and some of the steps will overlap in different ways. But, in general, the timeline roughly stays the same.

ADOPTION TIMELINE

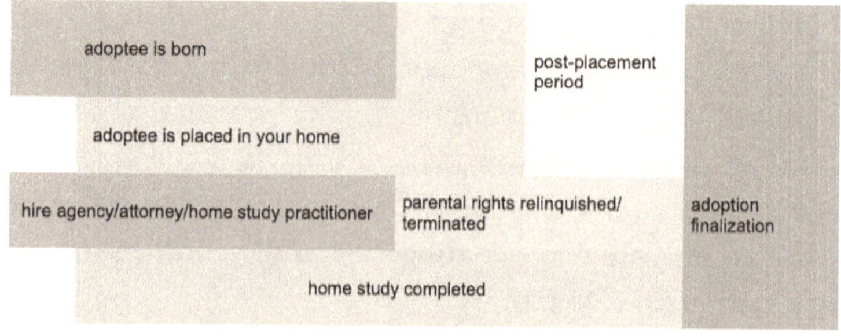

UNDERSTANDING ADOPTION THROUGH FOSTER CARE

Adopting a child from the foster care system will prescribe a different path than a private adoption. Let's look at your next steps if you were to choose adoption through foster care, also referred to as "foster to adopt."

Foster care is the placement of a child away from his/her biological parents (or legal guardians) due to substantiated child abuse, neglect, and/or exploitation until the parents/guardians resolve the issue(s) that removed the child from their care.

Typically, when a child enters the foster care system, the child's permanency plan will be reunification with their biological parents/legal guardians. You will serve as a team member alongside the CPS staff, biological parents, and the child in order to attempt to accomplish the child's plan of reunification. That might mean transporting the child to weekly visits with his biological parents or other court-ordered tasks. After a certain amount of time has passed (as determined by state statutes), if the parents/legal guardians have not remedied the issues that led to the child's removal from their care, the court may order that the child's permanency plan be changed from reunification to adoption. During this process, the CPS worker may have asked the child's other family members (grandparents, aunts, etcetera) if they would be willing and able to care for the child. If another family member is found to be appropriate and willing to care for the child, the child may be placed in their home with guardianship granted to that relative. The CPS case is then closed. If a fit and willing relative is not available, and the plan has changed to adoption, the CPS worker may ask the child's current foster parents if they are interested in adopting the child. If the child's foster parents decline, then the CPS worker will determine if another one of the department's home study-approved families would be a good fit for the child.

To get started with the foster to adopt path, contact your county's CPS office and let them know you are interested in adopting a child through foster care. Most likely, they'll schedule a time to meet with you to discuss their requirements and process. It is also likely that the CPS worker will encourage you to become a foster parent while you await a child with a plan of adoption.

If you are a CPS foster/adoptive family that is asked if you are interested in adopting a foster child, you have the right to decline or proceed with the process. If you decide to proceed, the CPS worker will arrange a meeting with you for Full Disclosure. Full Disclosure is a time when the CPS workers (who have been involved in this child's case since they were removed from their parents' care) give you all the information they have about the child, e.g., the reasons they came into foster care, their medical information, educational progress, and any concerns for mental, medical, or developmental health. Typically, after that Full Disclosure meeting, you have a determined period of time to review the information you've been provided, speak to the child's previous and current foster parents, consult with the child's medical providers, etcetera before you make another choice to continue the adoption process or stop at that point.

If you decide to continue, the CPS team and you will decide how to best transition the child into your home. This plan will also include when and how to tell the child that they are moving into an adoptive home. This transition plan will take into consideration the child's age and emotional maturity, the distance between the homes, the child's placement history, and anything else considered pertinent. The younger a child is, the quicker the move into their adoptive home will be. Older children require more time to adjust and develop trust with another family.

Once that child is formally placed in their adoptive home, the post-placement period begins. The CPS worker (who now may be referred to as your adoption worker) will visit you on a regular basis to ensure that all household members are adjusting well, and any concerns are addressed until the biological parental rights are relinquished/terminated and until the adoption is finalized in court. Most post-placement periods last six months before the adoption finalizes in court. At the finalization of the child's adoption, the adoptee's name can be changed, if desired, and the child's birth certificate will be modified to reflect the adoptee's new name and the adoptive parents will be listed as the parents. CPS will no longer be involved in your child's life.

UNDERSTANDING ADOPTION - DOMESTIC & INTERNATIONAL

Private adoption is simply the adoption of a child who is not in foster care. If you are interested in adopting privately, you can elect to go through an adoption agency or not. For an adoption to be legal (and not human trafficking), an attorney and a home study practitioner are required. An adoption agency typically conducts your home study and handles the legal requirements in addition to other potential services for the biological parents, such as counseling, and financial assistance. An adoption agency will facilitate the matching of the prospective adoptive family to the biological mother/adoptee. An adoption agency will continue to manage your adoption until the adoption finalization.

If you already know a biological parent who wants you to adopt their child, there is no need to go through an agency. You simply hire an attorney to file the legal documents and a home study practitioner to conduct your home study. Many prospective adoptive families also forgo an adoption agency and become "matched" with an expectant mother/adoptee by things like word of mouth, social media, and fundraising events.

With a private adoption, you can adopt from any US state or from another county. However, if you wish to adopt from another country, it is highly likely that you'll require an agency to ensure that every state/country's laws are satisfied. International Adoptions follow the same process in addition to abiding by the adoption laws of the child's country of origin, which can lengthen the process and add to your expenses. Many counties have joined The Hague Treaty on Intercountry Adoption and Co-operation in Respect of Intercountry Adoption (commonly referred to as The Hague Treaty). This treaty exists to protect "children, birth parents, and adopted parents and to prevent child trafficking and other abuses" (Davenport, 2006). Your agency will need to be "Hague accredited" if the country you want to adopt from is a member of the Hague Convention.

***Refer to Chapter 9 – Adoption Agencies for additional information.**

celebrating after a step-parent adoption finalization
court hearing

CHAPTER THREE

PROS AND CONS OF FOSTER TO ADOPT, PRIVATE DOMESTIC ADOPTIONS, AND INTERNATIONAL ADOPTIONS

As with any choice in life, there are pros and cons with each path available for your adoption journey. Here are some of the notable differences:

Foster to Adopt:
When adopting a child from foster care, the child is likely to be school-aged and part of a sibling group. It is important to keep in mind that every child in foster care has experienced abuse, neglect, abandonment, parental death, and/or exploitation to some degree and may have ongoing challenges due to those situations. In the Full Disclosure element of this adoption process, you will be told everything known about that child, such as any medical, educational, or mental health concerns for the child; this step allows you to make an informed self-evaluation to decide if you are able to provide the care needed/expected for this child. The state will pay for most, if not all, of your expenses for your adoption of a child in foster care. The state may also offer a monthly subsidy (until that child turns eighteen) to offset any expected, abnormal expenses you may face as you raise that child; the subsidy amount is determined by the child's expected need

for counseling, medical equipment, or for any other special needs. You are limited to being a foster parent to children in your state of residence. However, you can adopt a child from any state. You may have to travel to the child's city/state of residence. Adoptive parents may experience emotional fatigue when parenting a child that has experienced trauma. If the adoptive parent has unresolved trauma of their own, it may resurface.

Private Domestic Adoptions:
In domestic private adoptions, the majority of adoptees are newborns. Your knowledge of the background of an adoptee is limited to what the biological parents and/or the adoption agency disclose to you, so there may be unknown or undiagnosed conditions that are not discovered until later in that child's life. All expenses, fees from your attorney, home study practitioner, and/or adoption agency, and your travel expenses, will be out of your own pocket and there are no subsidies available in private adoptions. You can adopt from any state. You will have to travel to the state where and when the child is born and remain in that state until Interstate Compact on the Placement of Children (ICPC) grants you permission to leave the state with the adoptee. If you go through an adoption agency in another state, you will likely be traveling to that state when your adoptee is born since the biological parents are most likely from that same community.

The Interstate Compact on the Placement of Children (ICPC) is a "system that monitors the legal placement of children into foster care and adoption across state lines" (Pedley, 2010). If your adoptee resides (or is born) in a state other than your state of residence, ICPC will play a role in your adoption journey. For example, if you reside in New Mexico and the adoptee is born in Texas, your attorney and/or home study practitioner will coordinate with the Texas ICPC office so that you are able to return to your home in New Mexico with the child.

***Refer to Chapter 11 for more information on ICPC.**

International Adoptions:
The age of adoptees varies, but they will likely be school-aged children and not infants. Sibling groups may be available for adoption as well. There will be significant barriers to adopting a child from another country, such as culture, language, and religion. The history of a child is often unknown, so you may know little about their educational background, exposure to abuse/neglect/exploitation, mental/medical status, placement history, biological family, for example. There are usually no subsidies available for international adoptions. More expenses and a lengthier timeline are associated with international adoptions due to out-of-country travel and the involvement of multiple agencies/governments.

If you wish to adopt from another country, it is highly likely that you will need to go through an adoption agency to ensure that every state/country's laws are satisfied. International adoptions follow the same general process plus the laws of the child's country of origin, which can lengthen the process and add to your expenses. Many counties have joined The Hague Treaty on Intercountry Adoption and Co-operation in Respect of Intercountry Adoption (commonly referred to as The Hague Treaty). This treaty exists to protect "children, birth parents, and adopted parents and to prevent child trafficking and other abuses" (Davenport, 2006). Your agency will need to be "Hague accredited" if the country that you want to adopt from is a member of the Hague Convention.

family composed of two biological children and two
adopted children

prospective adoptive family

CHAPTER FOUR
RELINQUISHMENT OR TERMINATION OF PARENTAL RIGHTS

In order for a child to be adopted, that child first has to be "legally freed," meaning that the legal responsibilities of their biological parents have been ended in order for another adult (or adults) to assume that legal responsibility. Both biological parents' parental rights must be relinquished/terminated in order for a child to be legally freed for adoption. Until a child is legally freed for adoption, the adoption is considered a "legal risk" to the prospective adoptive parents since a biological parent could decide to parent the child. If a parent decides to parent their child and not place their child for adoption, then the child will be removed from the prospective adoptive home and returned to the biological parent's home. If a child is not legally freed for adoption, then that child cannot be adopted.

If the adoptee will be in your care prior to relinquishment or termination of the biological parents' rights, your attorney/agency will arrange for a Power of Attorney (POA), or another type of guardianship, to be in place. With that in place, you can leave the hospital with the adoptee (so it is not considered kidnapping), and make medical decisions for the child. A

POA is revocable and does not remove the parental rights from the child's biological parents.

The relinquishment/termination of parental rights might occur around the same time as your home study.

Relinquishment

Relinquishment is the voluntary choice to surrender your parental rights.

A parent can choose to relinquish their parental rights at nearly any point in their child's life. State law usually requires that a child is at least 48 hours old before a parent can legally relinquish their parental rights. State statutes will likely require that parents undergo "relinquishment counseling" beforehand with a qualified provider (typically a social worker or your home study practitioner) to ensure that the parent understands the ramifications of such an important decision, as it is irrevocable.

Termination

Termination of Parental Rights (TPR) is when a court removes the parental rights from a biological parent. Those hearings are often referred to as TPR hearings.

If a parent is unwilling to relinquish their parental rights and the attorney is able to prove to the court that the parent cannot appropriately parent the child, then the court may terminate the parent's parental rights. This situation may occur if a parent has previously had their parental rights to other children terminated.

There are many reasons a TPR may happen. For example, TPR may occur when a biological father is unknown or unable to be located. Initially, the attorney will be required to make sufficient efforts to identify or locate the father of the child. The biological mother may have to sign an affidavit regarding what information she knows or does not know about the biological father's identity and location. The attorney will publish public notices in places where the biological father may reside. The attorney will also verify that the alleged biological father is not listed on the Putative Father Registry. Every state has a provision, known as a Putative Father Registry, "for fathers to voluntarily acknowledge paternity or the possibility of paternity of a child born outside of a marriage" (adoptionart.org). Once those efforts have been exhausted, the court will terminate the biological father's parental rights, which is also irrevocable.

family's first photo with their internationally-adopted daughter finally at home on U.S. soil

CHAPTER FIVE
ADOPTEE COUNSELING

Some states will require adoptees of a certain age (usually ten years and older) to participate in adoptee counseling. Adoptee counseling occurs between the adoptee and a qualified individual, typically a social worker, home study practitioner, or CPS worker, depending on your particular adoption path. The social worker will ensure that the child understands what adoption is and if they want to be adopted by the prospective adoptive parent(s). The counseling session also allows the social worker to make sure the child understands that they can still love their biological parents and maintain a relationship with their biological family, as allowed by their adoptive parents. The adoptee must consent to their adoption; it is unlikely that an adoption will finalize without an adoptee's consent. The adoptee will also decide if their legal name will change. At the finalization of an adoption, the adoptee's name can be changed, if desired, and the child's birth certificate will be modified to reflect the adoptee's new name and the adoptive parents will be listed as the parents. To find an approved adoptee counseling provider, contact your attorney or ask your local CPS office if they maintain a list of approved providers.

family portrait taken after their step-parent
adoption finalization

You now know the basics of the adoption process. The first step is to decide what type of adoption best fits you (see chapter 2).

To find an attorney for your adoption journey, contact a local family law attorney.

To find a home study practitioner, ask your attorney or call your local CPS office to see if they maintain a list of approved home study practitioners for your state.

If you decide to go through an adoption agency, you will need to make that selection as well. Contact the agency of your choice; they will likely have an application to start services with them.

Do not be afraid to "shop around" for the professional that best fits your family's needs and makes you feel comfortable and confident in their skill set. Also, you can ask for recommendations from others that have adopted. Ask the professionals for references.

. . .

Once you have selected your adoption professionals/agency, you will need to begin your home study. A home study may take several months to complete, so you will want it to get it started as soon as you can. Your adoption professionals will guide you through the rest of your adoption journey.

family celebrating after their adoption finalization
court hearing

No matter what type of adoption path you choose, a home study will be required.

A home study is an intensive report compiled to ensure that the prospective adoptive family is suitable for the placement of a child. Due to the complexity of a home study, it may take several months to complete.

A home study includes home visits, interviews with household members, and criminal background checks from federal, state, and local agencies. Your child protective services (CPS) records will be pulled from your state(s) of residence for the last five years in order to comply with the Adam Walsh Child Protection and Safety Act. Your home study practitioner will also check the safety of your home and verify your income/resources, medical insurance, and automobile insurance. You may have to provide your home study practitioner with copies of birth/death certificates, marriage certificate(s), divorce decree(s), recent medical records for all household members, and pet vaccination records. Your home study practitioner will obtain references from individuals of your choice. You may be required to sign a weapons safety agreement if you own/keep weapons in the home or on your property.

Areas of strengths and concerns are addressed in a home study. Areas of concern address how the prospective adoptive parents currently function. For example, if a prospective adoptive parent suffered abuse as a child, the home study practitioner may detail how they have dealt with the abuse/abuser, how the abuse currently affects them, their knowledge of appropriate parenting and discipline, and the dynamics of current relationships. If the prospective adoptive couple has poor money management skills, then the home study practitioner may detail how they are working to improve their finances to become more financially stable. If the prospective adoptive parent had a substance abuse problem in their past, the home study practitioner may want to know when he/she last used the substance, how he/she copes with stress, and who composes their support system. Strengths will be noted in the home study as well. Strengths may include having a strong support system, being financially stable, having successfully worked through difficulties in your past, and having a positive attitude towards adoption.

Local, state, and federal criminal records will be collected as part of your home study. Checks for any CPS history will also be requested from all your states of residence for the last five years. A home study practitioner will most likely be unable to mitigate any of the following crimes: felony convictions for child abuse or neglect, felony convictions for spousal abuse, felony convictions for crime against children (including child pornography), a conviction for a crime involving violence, and/or a felony conviction within the past five years for physical assault, battery, or a drug-related offense, and thus the home study practitioner would deny approval of the home study.

A home study is valid for one year from its completion. If an adoption does not finalize before the home study expires, then the home study practitioner will conduct a home study update. Each subsequent home study update is valid for one year from its completion. *It is mandatory that your home study remain current and valid until the adoption finalizes.* A home study update is also necessary for major changes, such as a pregnancy or a change in employment or income.

If a prospective adoptive family has any major changes, they will need to inform their home study practitioner and attorney. These adoption professionals will arrange for the home study to be updated to reflect any changes, such as changes in residence, employment, income, childcare, community, and household members. Major changes will require a home study update even if the home study is not close to its one-year expiration. If you move to another state, your adoption professionals will involve ICPC or other adoption professionals as required by state and federal statutes. See Chapter 11 for more information on ICPC.

Until you have an approved home study, adoption agency/CPS staff will not disclose any details about an adoptee or consider you as a prospective adoptive placement for an adoptee.

Only a qualified individual, a home study practitioner, may conduct a home study. Your state statutes will dictate what those qualifications are. See chapter 6 for more information on locating a home study practitioner.

prospective adoptive parents holding their newborn
adoptee

family portrait of prospective adoptive parents with
their adoptee son and biological daughter

CHAPTER EIGHT
YOUR ATTORNEY AND OTHER LEGAL MATTERS

An attorney is a mandatory professional in your adoption journey. If you choose to foster to adopt or to adopt through an adoption agency, an attorney will most likely be on staff with that agency. If you do not utilize an adoption agency, you will need to hire an adoption or family law attorney.

The attorney will create and file all of your adoption legal documents, such as the petition for adoption, the relinquishment/termination of parental rights, and the adoption finalization.

If ICPC is involved, your attorney may liaise with the other state's ICPC office to arrange for your adoptee's entry into your state of residence. Refer to Chapter 11 for more information on ICPC.

Since a biological parent can not relinquish their parental rights until a child is at least 48 hours old, your attorney will arrange for the biological parent(s) to sign a Power of Attorney (POA) or temporary guardianship as soon as the baby is born. This legal document will allow you to make medical decisions in the hospital for the child and for the hospital staff to discharge the child from the hospital into your care. Ideally, this legal document will be in place until the biological parents' rights are terminated/relinquished.

From the time that the adoptee is legally freed for adoption until the adoption finalization, your attorney will have legal documents in place so that you have temporary guardianship of the child.

A child typically has to be placed in your home for six months before the adoption can be finalized in court. During this time, your home study practitioner will conduct mandatory post-placement visits and provide a post-placement report to your attorney. Once post-placement requirements have been fulfilled, your attorney will secure a court date for your adoption to be finalized. Refer to Chapter 13 for more information on the post-placement period and adoption finalization.

At the finalization hearing, the adoptee's name will be changed. In addition, you will now be able to modify the adoptee's birth certificate to reflect their new name and the adoptive parents' names as the child's parents.

There is no further involvement from any professionals or agencies after the finalization of your adoption!

prospective adoptive parents loving on their
newborn adoptee son

CHAPTER NINE
ADOPTION AGENCIES

If you decide to adopt through an adoption agency, you will need to choose the agency you want to hire. Adoption agencies vary in how they match prospective adoptive families to biological mothers, amongst other things, but they generally provide the same six services. These services include matching prospective adoptive parents with an adoptee, arranging relinquishment counseling for the biological parents, conducting the home study, providing education/support, preparing and filing the legal documents, and conducting the post-placement home visits. Some agencies only handle domestic adoptions and some may also offer international adoptions. Ongoing support groups for biological parents and adoptive families are often offered through adoption agencies.

You have the option to use an adoption agency in any state. You may choose an adoption agency in another state in order to lessen the likelihood that you know the adoptee's biological family. Whatever state that agency is located in is where you will most likely have to travel to when your adoptee is born or placed in your care. Often prospective adoptive families consider an agency within driving distance from their home or in a location where they can stay with family or friends until they can return home with their adoptee (see chapter 11 for more information on ICPC).

The adoption agency's expenses will be significant due to the services they provide. Most, if not all, of the adoption professionals you need will be on staff at an adoption agency. Think of an adoption agency as a one-stop-shop for you.

If you are interested in hiring an adoption agency, do not hesitate to shop around to find an agency that aligns with your lifestyle/beliefs and that you feel comfortable with. Look at their website. Ask the agency for references. Ask adoptive parents for recommendations. Find out what ages/countries an agency is licensed to conduct adoptions for. You might want to ask the following:

"How long has the agency existed?

What does the agency offer in terms of post-adoption support services?

What is the agency's experience in the type of adoption you want to pursue?

What is your average wait time?

How many waiting families are currently with your agency?

What requirements does the agency have for prospective adoptive parents?

What type of pre-adoption education does the agency provide?

How many children has your agency successfully placed within the last year?

How many of your placements have failed?" (adoptionformy-child.com)

prospective adoptive parents post photos on their social media accounts to keep their family and friends informed of their progress and to raise funds for their adoption expenses

Above are pages from a prospective adoptive family's book that was given to biological parents when they were selecting an adoptive family for their child. When working with an adoption agency, biological parents look through multiple family books in order to choose a family to adopt their child. This process does not apply to foster to adopt situations.

CHAPTER TEN

OPEN ADOPTIONS VERSUS CLOSED ADOPTIONS: THE DIFFERENCES AND THINGS TO CONSIDER

Closed adoption is where no information is shared and there is no contact between the biological family and the adoptive family. Open adoption is when the adoptive and biological families have access in varying degrees to each other's personal information in addition to the option of contact. Open adoption can mean simply that the adoptive family knows basic information about the adoptee's biological parents and that the adoptive family sends photos of the child to the biological parents through the adoption agency on a yearly basis. Or there can be a higher level of openness in an adoption. The adoptive parents may permit the biological parent(s) to maintain a close relationship with the adoptee. Open adoptions can be directly between the biological parents and the adoptive parents or the contact can be mediated by a third party (such as an adoption agency). Open adoptions may or may not include identifying information.

Do not confuse open adoption with co-parenting or a custody agreement. Those arrangements are different from open adoption. Arrangements for open adoption are set forth in the adoption finalization court order. However, there are no legal consequences if the adoptive parents opt to alter the openness, unlike in a child visitation arrangement that you would find in divorce or child custody hearings. Also, a biological parent cannot make open adoption a requirement in order for him/her to relinquish their parental rights. This erroneous thought should be addressed in the parent's relinquishment counseling session. *Adoptive parents can change the degree of openness as they feel is in the best interest of the child without any legal consequences no matter what open adoption arrangements were ordered in court.* (However, discuss your wishes with your attorney since adoptions statutes may vary state to state.)

The openness of an adoption can change over time and that is decided by the adoptive parents. Adoptive parents may decide that a biological parent's lifestyle choices are not appropriate or safe for them to maintain a relationship with their biological child. An adoptive parent may find that the adopted child has many questions about their biological roots and a relationship with a biological parent might be appropriate and meaningful to that child. A biological parent may get to a more stable time in their life when contact with the adopted child would be beneficial and appropriate.

Closed adoptions do not allow for a free flow of information between the adoptive parents and biological parents, which may include new medical information and the arrival of siblings. Biological parents have limited information about the adoptive family and may struggle with knowing that they selected the right family. Biological parents may not feel confident in the choice they made to place their child for adoption and the adoptive family selected. The adoptee will have little knowledge about their biological makeup and cultural roots, which may contribute to later struggles with their identity and sense of worth. Open adoptions allow for positive relationships with biological family members and the exchange of information between both parties as it benefits the adopted child. An adopted child will learn their biological roots/culture and may not struggle to the same degree with what circumstances led their biological parents to choose adoption for them. (Considering-Adoption.com)

ConsideringAdoption.com uses the following graphic to display the effects of open and closed adoption for adoptive parents, birth/biological parents, and adoptees:

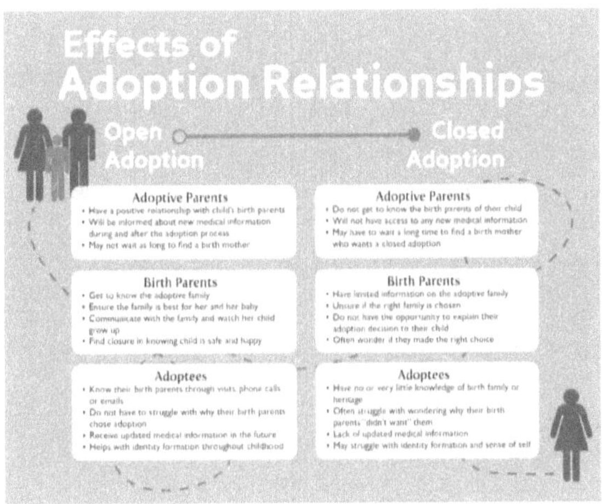

Research on Open and Closed Adoptions

The Minnesota Texas Adoption Research Project found six necessary factors to make an open adoption successful:

1. Shift in thinking from nuclear family to adoptive kinship network
2. Valuing of child's dual connection to birth and adoptive parents
3. Engaged participation across birth and adoptive sides of the network

4. Flexibility in day-to-day logistics
5. Excellent communication skills
6. Commitment to the relationship – in the best interest of the child

(https://openadoption.com/research-on-open-adoption/ accessed December 17, 2021)

CHAPTER ELEVEN
ICPC

The Interstate Compact on the Placement of Children (ICPC) is a "system that monitors the legal placement of children into foster care and adoption across state lines" (Pedley, 2010).

If your adoptee resides in a state other than your state of residence, ICPC will play a role in your adoption journey. For example, if you reside in New Mexico and the adoptee resides in Texas, your attorney and/or home study practitioner will coordinate with the Texas and New Mexico ICPC offices so that you are able to return to your home in New Mexico with the child.

As prospective adoptive parents in an ICPC-applicable adoption, be prepared for a potentially lengthy stay in the adoptee's state of origin while you await ICPC's approval for you and the child to proceed to your home state. Utilize that time to bond with your child and try not to worry about ICPC. Let your adoption professionals handle that matter. Your stay in another state may range from a few days to a month, depending on various factors, such as the timeliness of paperwork processed by the various agencies/professionals involved.

adoptive parents with their adopted twin daughters

CHAPTER TWELVE
ICWA

The Indian Child Welfare Act of 1978 (ICWA) "was passed in response to the alarmingly high number of Indian children being removed from their homes by both public and private agencies" (National Indian Child Welfare Association).

According to the National Indian Child Welfare Association, ICWA sets federal requirements that apply to state child custody proceedings involving an Indian child who is a member of or eligible for membership in a federally recognized tribe. ICWA applies in both foster care and adoption matters.

If you suspect that ICWA may apply to your situation, notify your adoption professionals so they can ensure that ICWA laws are followed. All tribes determine who is a citizen of their tribe and tribes have different eligibility requirements. For additional information, contact the Bureau of Indian Affairs.

When an adoptee is a Native American child, ICWA requires that the tribe be contacted and given preference as a placement resource for the child. If the tribe elects to not be involved, then the prospective adoptive family can proceed with their adoption journey.

To read The Indian Child Welfare Act of 1978, conduct an online search for "United States Code: Title 25."

prospective adoptive couple with their newborn
adoptee daughter

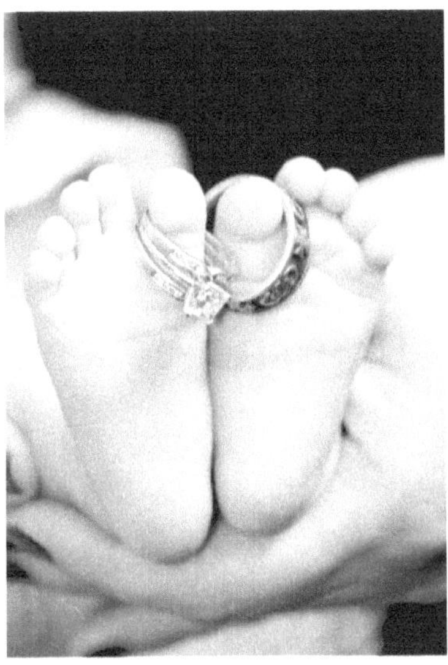

adoptee's feet with the prospective adoptive
couple's wedding rings

CHAPTER THIRTEEN
POST-PLACEMENT AND FINALIZATION

Post-placement refers to the time period starting when the adoptee is placed in an adoptive home until the adoption finalizes in court. In some states this time period lasts six months. However, a judge may waive this legal requirement in some situations, such as if the adoptee has been placed in the adoptive home for over six months already. The purpose of the post-placement period is to allow the adoptee, adoptive parents, and any other household members sufficient time to adjust to their new roles and have a successful adoption. During this post-placement period, the home study practitioner will make regular home visits to ensure that everyone in the household is adjusting well and that any concerns are addressed.

Six months is generally enough time that any developmental, medical, behavioral, educational, or other concerns may start to surface. The home study practitioner can assist the prospective adoptive family in navigating those new challenges before the adoption finalizes. In the event that those new challenges are unable to be resolved (or adequately addressed) and/or the prospective adoptive family decides that they are unable to parent the adoptee, the adoption professionals may move the adoptee to another prospective adoptive home to prevent a failed adoption. This situation is termed an adoption disruption or a failed adoption. If a child is removed from the adoptive parents' custody/care any time <u>after</u> adoption finalization, the adoptive parents could potentially face allegations of child abuse/neglect/exploitation/abandonment. The post-placement period is enacted in an attempt to avoid that scenario and to result in a successful adoption.

Near the end of the post-placement period, the home study practitioner will prepare a report for the attorney with the recommendation that the adoption be finalized. The attorney will file this post-placement report and schedule a court date. At the finalization court hearing, the judge will make the adoption final.

International adoptions may have different post-placement requirements. States may vary in their post-placement requirements as well. Your adoption professionals will know the requirements and will assist you in meeting each one in order to achieve a successful adoption.

After finalization, the adopted child's birth certificate can be changed to reflect their new name and to list the adoptive parents' names as if they were the child's biological parents. Also, the adoptive parents can add their adopted son/daughter to their medical insurance policies. Prior to that point, the adoptee should qualify for Medicaid, unless the insurance company allows you to add the adoptee while the adoption is still pending.

There will be no more involvement from your adoption professionals after the adoption finalization.

adoptive family with the judge after the adoption
finalization hearing

CHAPTER FOURTEEN

EXPENSES TO EXPECT IN THE ADOPTION PROCESS (AND HOW TO AFFORD ADOPTION)

The adoption of a foster child will incur minimal expenses. The state will pay for most, if not all, of your adoption expenses. The state may also offer a monthly subsidy (until that child turns eighteen) to offset any expected, abnormal expenses you may face as you raise that child. The amount is determined by the child's expected need for counseling, medical equipment, or any other special needs and will be determined prior to finalization.

International adoptions typically incur the most expenses since they involve a stateside agency (that may need to be a fully-accredited Hague agency), an agency in the adoptee's country of origin, travel expenses, and a lengthier timeline. Refer to Chapter 3 for more information on The Hague Treaty.

The involvement of an adoption agency for a domestic adoption will add a large expense to the adoption process. However, an adoption agency typically covers everything prospective adoptive parents need in addition to the needs of the biological parents. Fees will vary from agency to agency, so prospective adoptive parents may want to shop around to find the agency that they are comfortable with and that aligns with their lifestyle. Aside from the agency's fees, you may have travel and living expenses if the adoptee is located in another city/state.

If you are choosing a private domestic adoption without the involvement of an adoption agency, your expenses will consist of your traveling expenses in addition to the fees from your attorney and home study practitioner.

Affording Adoption

There are many ways to afford an adoption. You may choose to take out a bank loan. Or you can apply for adoption grants. Or you may host various fundraisers. Fundraisers may include selling T-shirts or baked goods or hosting a yard sale. Fundraising events range from drive-by diaper bombs - driving by the adoptive couple's home and tossing diapers full of cash at them - to selling puzzle pieces to your friends and family for them to "be a piece of your adoption journey." There are near-endless lists of creative ideas on social media sites, such as Pinterest.

The Adoption Tax Credit

"Tax benefits for adoption include both a tax credit for qualified adoption expenses paid to adopt an eligible child and an exclusion from income for employer-provided adoption assistance. The credit is nonrefundable, which means it's limited to your tax liability for the year. However, any credit in excess of your tax liability may be carried forward for up to five years. The maximum amount (dollar limit) for 2020 is $14,300 per child" (IRS, 2021). Typically, an adoption tax credit can only be claimed for the tax year in which the adoption finalizes. For more information, visit the IRS website or contact a certified public accountant (CPA).

Department of Defense (DoD) Adoption Reimbursement (also known as The Military Adoption Credit)

In 2022, the DoD offered a reimbursement for adoption expenses for United States active-duty military members for up to $2,000 per child in a calendar year with a maximum reimbursement amount of $5,000 per calendar year. Claims for reimbursement must be made no later than one year after the adoption is finalized. For more information, see Department of Defense Instruction 1341.09 or contact Military OneSource online at www.militaryonesource.mil or 1-800-342-9647.

Adoption Taxpayer Identification Number (ATIN)

According to the IRS, an ATIN is issued by the IRS as a temporary taxpayer identification number for the child in a domestic adoption where the adopting taxpayers do not have and/or are unable to obtain the child's Social Security Number (SSN). If you are in the process of adopting a child and are able to claim the adoptee as your dependent or you are able to claim them for a child care credit, you may need an ATIN for the adoptee. Some international adoptees may also qualify to get an ATIN. The IRS form titled "Form W-7A" is the "Application for Taxpayer Identification Number for Pending Adoptions," which is used by qualifying taxpayers to obtain an ATIN. For more information, visit the IRS website or contact your accountant.

Grants

There are a plethora of grants available to ease the financial load for adoptive parents. A simple Internet search will list many grants or you can ask other adoptive parents if they utilized an adoption grant.

adoptive family with the judge after the adoption
finalization court hearing.

CHAPTER FIFTEEN
GRIEF AND LOSS IN ADOPTION (AND TELLING YOUR CHILD THEY ARE ADOPTED)

Grief and Loss is a concept experienced by all travelers on an adoption journey. A biological parent is losing the opportunity or hope to parent their child. An adoptive parent may be dealing with infertility and, thus, the loss of experiencing pregnancy and childbirth. Not being raised by their biological family is a loss for an adoptee. These losses are just some that may be experienced.

"Losses must be acknowledged, validated, and grieved in order to heal and move forward. If losses are not grieved, the ongoing hurt and pain will negatively impact one's ability to function and form healthy attachments. Children grieve differently than adults, so it is important for adoptive parents to understand and identify how loss and grief manifest developmentally, behaviorally, and emotionally and learn strategies for helping children heal" (childwelfare.gov).

Kübler-Ross Grief Cycle

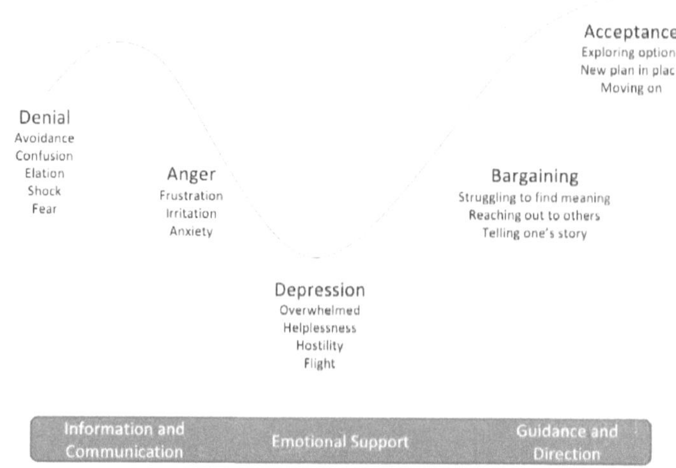

Published in <u>On Death and Dying</u>, the Elisabeth Kübler-Ross Theory of Grief offers emotional stages, as depicted in the image above. These stages often occur in this order, but it is also common for a person to jump around in the cycle repeatedly until, at last, reaching the final stage of acceptance.

Denial may look like this:

- My sisters were able to get pregnant, so I will conceive also.
- I can't afford to adopt.
- I would not make a good parent.
- You didn't adopt me; you/CPS kidnapped me.
- My dad didn't know my mom was pregnant with me or he would have come for me.
- If my biological father knew I existed, then he would have parented me.

- I can get my life in order so that I can parent my baby.
- I do not have a drug/alcohol problem.

Anger may look like this:

- The fertility doctor didn't know what he was doing.
- I hate my body.
- I am mad at my spouse for his/her infertility.
- You are not my mom/dad!
- CPS kidnapped my child.
- If he would not have convinced me to have sex, then I would not be dealing with an unplanned pregnancy.
- He/she should have used birth control.

Depression may look like this:

- I can't handle another negative pregnancy test.
- I am going to leave this marriage if we can't have a child.
- I do not want to spend time with my loved ones/friends/family; I want to seclude myself.
- I do not want to talk or think about my reproductive health.
- Having thoughts of suicide, of not existing anymore, or of physically hurting yourself or others.
- Having no motivation to do activities that you used to enjoy doing.
- I do not want to participate in our open adoption arrangements.
- I do not want to acknowledge that I placed my child for adoption.

Bargaining may look like this:

- If I would have led a healthier lifestyle, I could have conceived.
- If I would have behaved, then my biological parent would have parented me.
- If we would have tried to have children when we were younger, then we could have conceived.
- If I had the support from my family/partner, I could have parented my child.
- If CPS would have not gotten involved, I would still have custody of my child.

Acceptance may look like this:

- I placed my first-born child for adoption and I am very proud of his/her parents.
- I love my biological parents and my adoptive parents.
- Our child's biological parents are brave and unselfishly love our child.
- Let us share how adoption shaped our family.

"Telling a child he is adopted is more of a process than an event. Talking to a child about adoption starts when he is quite young, often continuing until he is a teenager or adult." (Alexander, 2004).

An adopted child will likely reach acceptance easier and sooner if their adoptive parents discuss their adoption story with them from the day that child enters their home. As difficult as it may be, it will greatly benefit everyone if the adoption journey is shared and not hidden.

There are many great resources such as support groups, websites, books, social workers, and counselors to aid adoptive parents in talking to their adopted child about their adoption. Adoptive parents will need to take into consideration the child's developmental age and emotional maturity. Listen to your adopted child and allow them to ask questions. Do not hesitate to be honest with your child, even about the not-so-pretty parts of your child's past. Your child will learn that you have chosen to accept and love him/her despite the "ugly" parts of their background, and as a result, their trust and love for you will increase.

Open adoptions can help facilitate healthier movement through the grief cycle. Children may be more likely to have their questions answered directly by biological family members when open adoption is in place. See Chapter 10 for more information on open and closed adoptions.

***See "Adoption and the Stages of Development" by Child Welfare Information Gateway in the Appendix for more information.**

CHAPTER SIXTEEN
SAFE HAVEN

"Many state legislatures have enacted legislation to address infant abandonment and endangerment" (Children's Bureau, 2016) thus creating safe haven laws. "Since 1999, infant safe haven laws have been enacted as an incentive for mothers in crisis to safely relinquish their babies to designated locations where the babies are protected and provided with medical care until a permanent home is found. Safe haven laws generally allow the parent to remain anonymous and to be free from criminal charges for child endangerment, abandonment, or neglect in exchange for surrendering their baby to a safe haven" Children's Bureau, 2016.) Safe Haven laws vary state to state (and may even vary from county to county).

Designated locations are usually hospitals, fire departments, and police stations. Once a baby is left at a designated location, the medical professionals/first responders immediately ensure the baby's safety and provide medical care, shelter, and nourishment.

The local child protective services (CPS) agency will gain custody of the child and will look to place the baby into a prospective adoptive home as quickly as possible. CPS will petition the court for termination of the biological parent's parental rights.

For more information or if you are interested in being a prospective adoptive family for a safe haven baby, contact your local CPS office. If you are interested in using the safe haven law to place your newborn for adoption, contact any designated location to verify any age requirements for the baby.

family at their adoption finalization court hearing

CHAPTER SEVENTEEN
STEP-PARENT ADOPTIONS

If you have a child from a previous relationship and desire for your current spouse to adopt your child, then you are considering a step-parent adoption. In order for your spouse to adopt your child (their stepchild), then the parental rights of the child's non-custodial parent must be terminated or relinquished. Keep in mind that once the paternal rights of a non-custodial parent are ended, then that parent will no longer be required to pay child support or have visitations. A home study, adoptee counseling, couples counseling, relinquishment counseling, and/or step-parent counseling may be required depending on your state statutes. To find out more information or to get started, contact a local family attorney, who will know the requirements and process to initiate your step-parent adoption. Also, note that a step-parent adoption typically does not qualify for an adoption tax credit with the IRS or DoD.

father with his children after the step-parent
adoption finalization court hearing

You may be struggling with your decision to adopt. It's not uncommon to question why God wouldn't give you a biological child. But I encourage you to remember adoption is a beautiful thing that should be celebrated. God literally gave us adoption as a gift.

Adoption is God's idea and He models this concept in His adoption of believers as His children. God sent His only Son to Earth as a sacrifice for mankind to have the opportunity to receive forgiveness for our sins and to have a relationship with God. Once a person accepts and believes this truth, they are a Christian and are adopted as a son or daughter of God. Adoption is one of the metaphors used in the Bible to explain how Christians are brought into the family of God.

The Bible is God's inerrant word to mankind. Look at these references about adoption:

Psalms 68:5 (NIV) A father to the fatherless, a defender of widows, is God in his holy dwelling.

Psalms 82:3 (NIV) Defend the weak and the fatherless; uphold the cause of the poor and the oppressed.

Psalm 139:13-16 (NIV) For you created my inmost being; you knit me together in my mother's womb. I praise you because I am fearfully and wonderfully made; your works are wonderful, I know that full well. My frame was not hidden from you when I was made in the secret place, when I was woven together in the depths of the earth. Your eyes saw my unformed body; all the days ordained for me were written in your book before one of them came to be.

Jeremiah 1:5 (NIV) "Before I formed you in the womb I knew you, before you were born I set you apart; I appointed you as a prophet to the nations."

Galatians 4:4-5 (NIV) But when the set time had fully come, God sent his Son, born of a woman, born under the law, to redeem those under the law, that we might receive adoption to sonship.

Ephesians 1:4-5 (NIV) For he chose us in him before the creation of the world to be holy and blameless in his sight. In love he predestined us for adoption to sonship through Jesus Christ, in accordance with his pleasure and will.

Matthew 1:18 (NIV) This is how the birth of Jesus the Messiah came about: His mother Mary was pledged to be married to Joseph, but before they came together, she was found to be pregnant through the Holy Spirit.

Romans 8:15 (NIV) The Spirit you received does not make you slaves, so that you live in fear again; rather, the Spirit you received brought about your adoption to sonship. And by him we cry, "Abba, Father."

Romans 8:17 (NIV) Now if we are children, then we are heirs – heirs of God and co-heirs with Christ, if indeed we share in his sufferings in order that we may also share in his glory.

Romans 8:23 (NIV) Not only so, but we ourselves, who have the firstfruits of the Spirit, groan inwardly as we wait eagerly for our adoption to sonship, the redemption of our bodies.

James 1:27 (NIV) Religion that God our Father accepts as pure and faultless is this: to look after orphans and widows in their distress and to keep oneself from being polluted by the world.

I John 3:1 (NIV) See what great love the Father has lavished on us, that we should be called children of God! And that is what we are! The reason the world does not know us is that it did not know him.

CHAPTER NINETEEN
MILITARY AND ADOPTION

The United States military is a unique population. They move all over the world, deploy, train, share an exclusive culture, and gain experiences that are highly uncommon for civilians. Thus, the military member is often wrongly thought of as a poor resource for a child. If you and/or your spouse is a military member, do not let that hamper your desire to adopt. The process of adoption is the same for military families, as it is not a different type of adoption. Sometimes military adoptions require the home study professionals to work around deployments and other military-specific events.

Sometimes adoption professionals simply need some gentle education on the lifestyle of military families in order to see the benefits of a child growing up in a military family. If you do not feel comfortable advocating for yourself with adoption professionals, seek support from your resiliency resources on your installation. For example, in the United States Air Force (USAF), the Airman & Family Readiness Center (AFRC) or the School Liaison Officer (SLO) may be able to support you. Military OneSource also has many adoption-related resources. Military counselors can also support. These military-specific resources can help you troubleshoot any concerns that arise so that you can comfortably and effectively address your situation with the involved adoption professionals.

Here are some special considerations for the military member's home study:

- Who composes your support system when the active-duty member is deployed?

- Who can you rely on in an emergency to care for your child?

- What are your childcare arrangements when you are at work?

- Will you have a POA or Last Will in place after the adoption finalization?

- As a single parent active-duty member, what arrangements will you have in place when you deploy or have to work later than planned?

- How far away does your extended family live?

- How often do you have a permanent change of station (PCS)?

- How often do you deploy?

- Do you expect to PCS any closer to your extended family or to an overseas installation?

Many wonderful resources are available to military families. Military members have exceptional medical coverage with Tricare. Even after a military member retires, the family will retain this medical coverage, at little or no cost. Upon placement of an adoptee, the active-duty member can apply/enroll the adoptee in the Exceptional Family Member Program (EFMP) with the United States Department of Defense. The EFMP works with other military and civilian agencies in order to provide comprehensive and coordinated community support, housing, educational, medical, and personnel services worldwide to US military families with special needs. With the EFMP, the military will not move the active-duty member and their family to a duty station where they do not have access to the services that they need for their family. Lastly, as a military member, there are many free resources that are available to the family through Military OneSource such as respite care, adoption services, mental health counseling, financial services, health and wellness coaching, and referral services. (Contact Military OneSource for more information.)

If a prospective adoptive family plans to move to another installation (known as a PCS) before their adoption is finalized, they will need to let their home study practitioner and attorney know. These adoption professionals will arrange for the home study to be updated to reflect the changes in residence, employment, childcare, community, etc. Any major changes, such as moving, requires a home study update in order to keep your home study active and valid until adoption finalization. In addition, your adoption professionals will involve ICPC or other adoption professionals as required by state and federal statutes.

prospective adoptive family

If you are pregnant (or your partner is pregnant), you may be considering making a plan of adoption for your child. If you have looked at the previous chapters, you have learned the process from an adoptive parent's standpoint. Let's look at what the process might look like from your perspective.

At any point during your pregnancy or after your child is born, you can make a plan of adoption for your child. Your child can be a newborn, four years old, ten years old, or seventeen years old; it does not matter as long as your child has not reached the age of majority.

If you decide that you cannot parent your child, you have up to four options:

1) You can choose to place your child for adoption through an adoption agency. An adoption agency will have home study-approved families to be matched with your child. Adoption agencies will allow you, if you want, to play a major part in selecting your child's adoptive family. Adoption agencies will also assist in creating a plan for open adoption, if you want that.

Adoption agencies may be able to offer you some financial assistance during your pregnancy; they may also offer ongoing support or counseling.

2) If you do not want to involve an adoption agency, you can ask anyone if they are interested in adopting your child. Sometimes biological parents have a family member or friend that they trust and want to adopt their child. That individual/couple would still have to complete an approved home study and involve an attorney in order to legally adopt your child.

3) If you are unable to parent your child, but are not interested in a plan of adoption for your child, you may elect to put a Power of Attorney (POA) or another form of guardianship in place. These legal documents would extend parental rights to another person without terminating your parental rights. You can elect to revoke these legal documents at any time.

4) Depending on your child's age, you can surrender your child at an identified Safe Haven location. Your child would be in CPS custody and that agency would make the plans for permanency for your child without your input. Refer to chapter 16 for more information on Safe Haven.

If you are a non-custodial parent, you may be considering allowing your child's step-parent to adopt them. If you relinquish your parental rights or have your parental rights terminated, you would no longer have court-ordered visitations/contact. Any contact or involvement you would have with your biological child, would be at the discretion of their custodial parent and adoptive parent. You would not have to pay any delinquent or future child support payments once your parental rights are relinquished or terminated. Your biological child would no longer be able to inherit from you without a Last Will in place once those parental rights are removed. If you were to die while your child is still a minor, he/she would not be able to claim a Social Security death benefit. You may be required to participate in relinquishment counseling with a qualified professional before the court will accept your relinquishment.

If Child Protective Services (CPS) has custody of your child, your child's permanency plan will be decided by CPS and/or the court. If you are unable to regain custody of your child, you may have the option to assist CPS in locating appropriate and willing relatives to care for your child. However, any final decision would be made by CPS or the court since those entities have custody of your child. If this is your situation, discuss your options with your attorney.

- ***Can I adopt as an unmarried adult? Or as an older adult?***

Most likely, yes, but you will need to review your state statutes on adoption (or speak with your attorney) to verify any requirements such as marital status or age.

- ***Will I be able to continue the adoption process (or be allowed to stop the adoption process) if I become pregnant?***

When you begin your home study process, let your home study practitioner know if you are using birth control and/or are still involved in fertility treatments. Your home study practitioner will discuss with you your wishes to continue your home study if you were to get pregnant, how you would parent multiple children at the same time, and whether you and your family members would treat the biological child and adopted child differently.

- ***Will my criminal record keep me from adopting?***

Be open and honest with your home study practitioner about your charges/convictions. State statutes will determine what offenses can be mitigated and what charges/convictions cannot be overlooked. Such non-negotiable criminal background results may include: felony convictions for child abuse or neglect, felony convictions for spousal abuse, felony convictions for crime against children (including child pornography), a conviction for a crime involving violence, and/or a felony conviction within the past five years for physical assault, battery, or a drug-related offense. Local, state, and federal records will be requested for every adult household member. In addition, CPS records will be reviewed from every state resided in during the last 5 years.

- ***Does my home have to be spotless and child-proofed to pass a home study?***

No. Your home study practitioner will likely expect a certain level of cleanliness, but will be more concerned with the prospective adoptive parents' attitudes and cooperation during the home study process. Speak to your home study practitioner about what baby-safety features you are expected to have in your home. Most likely your home study practitioner is not going to require you to purchase every baby safety product on the market. For example, if you are expecting a newborn to be placed in your home, you may be required to have an appropriate sleeping space, such as a crib, in your home by the completion of your home study. It might be unnecessary to have a baby gate until the baby is starting to crawl. There may be safety requirements that have to be met during your home study, such as keeping a fire extinguisher in the kitchen or installing smoke detectors in the bedrooms. State statutes may dictate what safety features are required in an adoptive home.

- ***Will my medical/mental health condition prevent me from passing my home study?***

Probably not. Speak openly and honestly with your home study practitioner about your medical and mental health diagnoses and how you manage those condition(s). Your home study practitioner may discuss with you how the placement of a child in your home may impact those conditions.

- ***How long will it take to adopt a child?***

State statutes may dictate a deadline for your home study to be completed. For a domestic adoption, you may look at a home study taking a few months to complete and then a varied amount of time to wait for the placement of an adoptee. Once an adoptee is placed in your home, the post-placement period begins, which typically lasts six months, and then the adoption will finalize. The timeline for an international adoption will be longer. Speak with your adoption professionals to find out what the average time is from starting the home study process to the adoption finalization.

Exceptions to the Rules

Since there are many paths to adoption, there are also exceptions to every "rule." For example, post-placement requirements can be waived by a judge. You could choose to file pro se, meaning that you file the legal documents yourself, without an attorney. You may make a random connection through an acquaintance that ultimately connects you with an adoptee. Always talk to your adoption professionals about your situation, issues, concerns, and preferences.

Scams

Unfortunately, people prey on those desperate to parent a child. As a hopeful adoptive parent, you should be very leery of providing your personal information or financial assistance to an expectant parent without the involvement of adoption professionals. Additionally, be cautious of what information you put on social media. The best way to avoid scams is to involve licensed, qualified adoption professionals in your adoption journey.

Safety Considerations

If you already have children in your home, you will need to consider their safety and well-being when you consider what child characteristics would be a good fit in your family. An adopted child may have additional emotional, medical, or mental health needs. For example, you may not want to consider adopting an older child who has suffered severe sexual abuse if you have younger children already in your home. You may not feel that you are able to devote the time needed to parent multiple children in your home, especially if one or more of your children have any special needs. Considerations for various child characteristics will likely be discussed during your home study.

Risks

It is important to keep in mind that there are inherent financial and emotional risks associated with every adoption. As with all adoptions, there are risks and unknown factors involved that may prevent a successful adoption. You may find it beneficial to consult with an attorney, an adoption consultant, a home study practitioner, other adoptive parents, or adoption support groups about the risks and concerns associated with adoption.

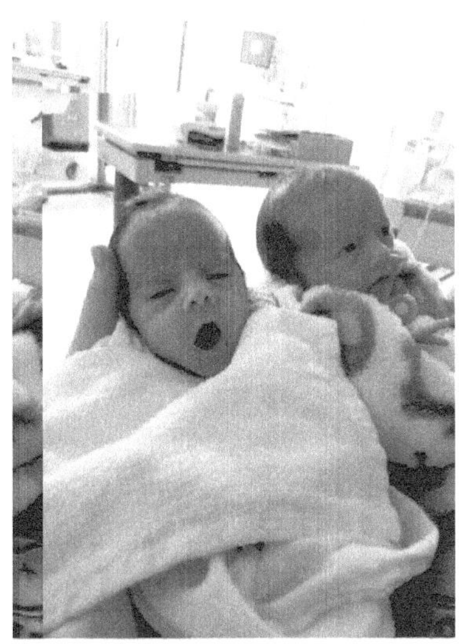

twin girls in the arms of their prospective adoptive
parents shortly after their births

Adoptee – a child with a permanency plan of adoption. "The person who was adopted" (Adamec, 2004).

Adoption – "the complete transfer of parental rights and obligations from one family to another family" (Adamec, 2004).

Adoption disruption – the term for when, before adoption finalization, challenges are unable to be resolved (or adequately addressed) and/or the adoptive family decides they are unable to parent the adoptee, so the adoptee is moved to another prospective adoptive home. Also known as a failed adoption.

Adam Walsh Child Protection and Safety Act of 2006 – established "a comprehensive national system for the registration of sex offenders and offenders against children" (congress.gov). Adam Walsh Child Protection and Safety Act of 2006 requires that a home study practitioner check the CPS records for states of residence for the last 5 years.

Biological parents – also referred to as birth parents.

Closed adoption – a form of adoption where the biological and adoptive families have no access to each other's personal information and do not have any contact with each other after adoption finalization.

CPS – child protective services; a state government agency designed to protect children; see foster care.

Failed adoption – term for when, before adoption finalization, challenges are unable to be resolved (or adequately addressed) and/or the adoptive family decides they are unable to parent the adoptee, so the adoptee is moved to another prospective adoptive home; also known as adoption disruption.

Foster care – system for when a child cannot safely reside in their parents' custody so a state government agency (CPS) gains custody of the child; see CPS.

Foster to adopt – term used for adopting a child from the foster care system.

Full Disclosure – in this part of the foster to adopt adoption process, the prospective adoptive parents will be told everything known about the adoptee, such as any medical, educational, or mental health concerns for the child; this step allows for an informed decision as to whether or not you are able to provide the care needed/expected for this child.

Hague Treaty on Intercountry Adoption and Co-operation in Respect of Intercountry Adoption - commonly referred to as The Hague Treaty. This treaty protects "children, birth parents, and adopted parents and to prevent child trafficking and other abuses" (Davenport, 2006).

Home study - an intensive report compiled to ensure that the prospective foster/adoptive family is suitable for the placement of a child or a sibling group.

Home Study Practitioner - a qualified/licensed individual who conducts the home study, typically a licensed social worker; the requirements to be a home study practitioner are set by state's statutes.

Interstate Compact on the Placement of Children (ICPC) - the mandatory legal process used to place a child from one state to another for purposes of foster care and/or adoption. It was enacted to ensure protection and services for foster/adoptive children who are placed in another state.

Indian Child Welfare Act of 1978 (ICWA) - a federal law passed in 1978 in response to the alarmingly high number of Indian children being removed from their homes by both public and private agencies; the intent of Congress under ICWA was to "protect the best interests of Indian children and to promote the stability and security of Indian tribes and families" (25 U.S.C. § 1902); ICWA sets federal requirements that apply to state child custody proceedings involving an Indian child who is a member of or eligible for membership in a federally recognized tribe.

International adoption – adoption from a country other than your country of residence.

Legal guardian – a person legally responsible for a child, but parental rights are still in place; a legal guardianship can be revoked by the parent.

Legal risk – parental rights are not yet terminated/relinquished for a child with a plan of adoption.

Legally freed for adoption – parental rights have been terminated or relinquished for a child with a plan of adoption.

Military Adoption Credit – See www.dfas.mil/MilitaryMembers/payentitlements/adoptionreimbursement for more information or call Military One Source at 1-800-342-9647.

NIV – New International Version – a contemporary English version of the Bible translated by more than one hundred scholars working from the best available Hebrew, Aramaic, and Greek texts.

Open adoption - a form of adoption where the biological and adoptive families have access to varying degrees of each other's personal information and have the option of various forms of contact after the finalization of the adoption; the adoptive family has the final say in the degree of openness.

Parental rights – rights and responsibilities to make decisions and to take appropriate actions for a child's upbringing.

Placement – home/facility where a child has resided.

PCS – a military term that stands for a Permanent Change of Station; when an active-duty member moves to another duty station.

Power of Attorney (POA) - a legal document that is put in place by a parent that grants authority to a person to make decisions on the parent's behalf for a child; does not terminate the parent's parental rights; can be revoked by the parent who put the POA in place.

Private adoption – adoption of a child that is in the care/custody of a biological parent and not in foster care; does not refer to a form of privacy or confidentiality.

Prospective adoptive parent – an adult that is hoping/planning to adopt, but the adoption has not yet finalized.

Putative father registry - a state level legal option for unmarried men to document through a notary public any woman they engage with in intercourse for the purpose of retaining parental rights for any child they may have fathered (Child Welfare, Information Gateway, 2010).

Relinquishment - the voluntary choice to surrender your parental rights.

Safe Haven Law – statutes in US states/counties that allow for a parent to surrender their newborn at a safe location and not face any criminal charges; the child becomes a ward of the state (enters foster care) and is placed into a prospective adoptive home.

Social worker – a trained and licensed professional that helps others that are in a disadvantaged situation; has a bachelor's and/or master's degree in social work and is licensed in their state(s) of practice.

Statute – a law.

Subsidy – a financial incentive, such as a monthly subsidy given to parents who adopt a child from the foster care system.

Tax credit - "a tax incentive which allows certain taxpayers to subtract the amount of the credit they have accrued from the total they owe the state. It may also be a credit granted in recognition of taxes already paid or a form of state 'discount' applied in certain cases. Another way to think of a tax credit is as a rebate." (Wikipedia, 2021).

Termination of Parental Rights (TPR)- termination is when a court removes the parental rights from a parent; those hearings are often referred to as TPR hearings.

sibling group announcing their family's plan to adopt
internationally

RESOURCES

Academy of Adoption and Assisted Reproduction Attorneys. *Putative Father Registries. Retrieved December 17, 2021, from https://adoptionart.org/adoption/birth-expectant-parents/putative-father-registries*

Adamec, Christine. (2004). The Complete Idiot's Guide to Adoption: Straightforward Advice to Guide you Through Every Stage of the Adoption Process. New York, New York. Penguin Group Inc.

Adoption for my Child. *How to Prepare for an Adoption Home Study, Home Visit, Interviews, and More.... Retrieved December 202 from https://www.adoptionformychild.com/home-study/*

Alexander, Christopher J. (2004). Welcome Home. Albuquerque, New Mexico. Mountain West Publishing.

Bible Study Tools. *Bible Verses about Adoption. Retrieved: December 15, 2021, from https://www.biblestudytools.com/search*

Child Welfare Information Gateway. (30 June 2010.) *The Rights of Unmarried Fathers* [brochure] n.p.: U.S. Department of Health and Human Services.

Child Welfare Information Gateway. *Grants/Loans/Tax Credits for Adoption.* Retrieved December 21, 2021, from https://www.childwelfare.gov/topics/adoption/adoptive/expenses/grants-loans/

Child Welfare Information Gateway. *Helping Adopted Children Cope with Grief and Loss. Retrieved December 19, 2021 from: https://www.childwelfare.gov/topics/adoption*

Child Welfare Information Gateway with the Children's Bureau. (December 2016). "Infant Safe Haven Laws" [brochure]. n.p.: U.S. Department of Health and Human Services.

Congress.Gov. *H.R.4472 - Adam Walsh Child Protection and Safety Act of 2006.* Retrieved December 5, 2021 from www.congress.gov/bill/109th-congress/house-bill/4472

Considering Adoption. *Effects of Adoption Relationships.* Retrieved November 21, 2021 from https://consideringadoption.com/wp-content/uploads/2015/11/Effects-of-Adoption-Relationships-Graphic.jpg

Considering Adoption. *Open vs. Closed Adoption - An Honest Comparison.* Retrieved December 27, 2021 from https://consideringadoption.com/adopting/open-adoption/open-vs-closed-adoption-an-honest-comparison/

Davenport, Dawn. (2006). <u>The Complete Book of International Adoption: A Step-by-Step Guide to Finding Your Child</u>. New York: Broadway Books.

Got Questions. *What does the Bible say about adoption?* Retrieved January 2, 2022 from https://www.gotquestions.org/adoption.html

Holy Bible. *Search results for Bible.* Retrieved December 1, 2021 from https://www.bible.com/search/bible?q=adoption

Internal Revenue Service. *Adoption Taxpayer Identification Number.* Retrieved December 21, 2021 from https://irs.gov/individuals/adoption-taxpayer-identification-number

Internal Revenue Service. *Topic No. 607 Adoption Credit and Adoption Assistance Programs. Retrieved January 3, 2022 from https://www.irs.gov/taxtopics/tc607*

Kübler-Ross. *Grief Cycle.* Retrieved December 19, 2021 https://i2.wp.com/www.grandofdublin.com/wp-content/uploads/2019/08/kubler-ross.jpg

National Indian Child Welfare Associate. *The Indian Child Welfare Act: A Family's Guide. Retrieved December 5, 2021 from https://www.nicwa.org/wp-content/uploads/2017/04/The-Indian-Child-Welfare-Act-A-Familys-Guide.pdf*

Minnesota Texas Adoption Research Project. *The Texas to Minnesota Adoption Research Project: Navigating Contact from Childhood into Young Adulthood.* Retrieved December 31, 2021 from http://psych.umass.edu/adoption/

Military OneSource. *EFMP: Exceptional Family Member Program.* Retrieved January 3, 2022 from https://www.militaryonesource.mil/family-relationships/special-needs/exceptional-family-member/

Pedley, Jennifer Joyce. (2010). <u>Secrets to Your Successful Domestic Adoption: Insider Advice to Create Your Forever Family Faster.</u> Deerfield Beach, Florida: Health Communications.

Pertman, Adam. (2011). <u>Adoption Nation: How the Adoption Revolution is Transforming Our Families and America.</u> Boston, Massachusetts: Harvard Common Press.

U.S. Department of the Interior Indian Affairs. *Indian Child Welfare Act (ICWA)*. Retrieved January 3, 2022 from https://www.bia.gov/bia/ois/dhs/icwa

USAACE & Fort Rucker Preventative Law Program. (March 27, 2015.) *Adoption Expense Reimbursement* [brochure] Fort Rucker, Alabama.

ABOUT THE AUTHOR

Stacy Gleaton is a Licensed Clinical Social Worker (LCSW) in New Mexico and Texas. She has worked in multiple social work settings over the years. One such social work job was with Child Protective Services (CPS) in New Mexico, where she first professionally learned about foster care and adoption. Stacy then continued to conduct home studies, but this time in the private sector. In 2015, Stacy began working with the military population and found it to be generally mistaken as a poor resource for an adoptive family; she enjoys advocating for military families in their adoption journey. As a Christian, Stacy has found many similarities between adoption and her relationship with God.

It is her hope that this book will give you the comfort and competence needed to begin your adoption journey!

Stacy loves to hear and learn from adoptive families, so please email her at Stacy.LCSW@gmail.com.

APPENDIX

Child Welfare
Information Gateway

PROTECTING CHILDREN ■ STRENGTHENING FAMILIES

1990

Adoption and the Stages
of Development

Now that you have adopted a child and life is beginning to settle down, you may find your thoughts moving to the future. When shall I tell my child that s/he is adopted? How will s/he feel about it? At what point will s/he want more information? What will s/he want to know from me? How can I help my child feel comfortable about being adopted?

What's Inside:

- The first year
- The second year
- Ages 2 to 6
- Elementary school years
- Adolescence
- When you need help

U.S. Department of Health and Human Services
Administration for Children and Families
Administration on Children, Youth and Families
Children's Bureau

Child Welfare Information Gateway
Children's Bureau/ACYF
1250 Maryland Avenue, SW
Eighth Floor
Washington, DC 20024
703.385.7565 or 800.394.3366
Email: info@childwelfare.gov
www.childwelfare.gov

Whether children are adopted as infants or when they are older, whether they are healthy or have physical or psychological problems, their adoption is bound to influence their development. You need to understand how and why.

Learning about the developmental stages of children and what can be expected in each stage is important to all new parents. When your child has been adopted, there are additional considerations. In these pages, we will be looking at specific issues—separation, loss, anger, grief, and identity—and show how they are expressed as your adopted child grows up. Some of these issues will be obvious in all stages of development; others surface at specific times. The more thoroughly you can understand how your child behaves and why, the more likely it is that you can be supportive and help your child to grow up with healthy self-esteem and the knowledge that s/he is loved.

While the stages described below correspond generally to a child's chronological age, your child's development may vary significantly. Some children progress more quickly from one stage to another; others may continue certain behaviors long past the time you would have expected. Still others may be substantially delayed in entering and moving through new stages. Many characteristics of adolescence, for instance, may not even appear until your child's twenties and may persist until your child's identity has formed.

The First Year

The primary task of a baby is to develop a sense of trust in the world and come to view it as a place that is predictable and reliable. Infants accomplish this through attachment to their caretakers. During their early months, children have an inborn capacity to "bond" to ensure their survival. They express it through sucking, feeding, smiling, and cooing, behaviors which, ideally, stimulate loving responses from their parents (or caretakers). These pleasant interactions and the parent's or parents' consistent attention form the parent-child bond and the foundation for a child's sense of trust.

During this period, a consistently nurturing and tension-free environment makes a child feel secure. The most valuable thing you can do is to show, through attention and affection, that you love your child and that your child can depend on you. If you generally respond to your child's cries, s/he will learn trust. If you hug and smile at your child, s/he will learn to feel content.

Although the need to attach continues for a long time, the process of separation also begins in the first year of a child's life. A milestone is reached when children learn to separate from their parents by crawling and then by walking. At the same time, babies often become fearful of separation. Psychological separation begins too: babies start, non-verbally, to express their own wishes and opinions. Many experts in child development view early childhood as a series of alternating attachment and separation phases that establish the child as an independent person who can relate happily to family members and friends, and be capable of having intimate relationships with others.

The Second Year

Toddlers continue the attachment and separation cycle in more sophisticated ways in the second year. They learn to tell you how they feel by reaching their arms out to you and protesting vigorously when you must leave them. Anxiety about separating from you heightens, and they may begin to express anger. During this stage, when you must guide and protect your child, you become a "no" sayer. It is not surprising that your child becomes frustrated and shows it in new ways. Helpless crying usually comes first. Later your child may exhibit aggressive behavior such as throwing things, hitting, pushing, biting, and pinching. Much of this behavior is directed toward you but some is directed at the child's peers. Such behavior often puzzles and frightens parents. You may wonder if your child is normal. Adoptive parents often worry that an unknown genetic trait is surfacing or that the "orneriness" has something to do with the adoption. Sometimes they think ahead to the teenage years and wonder if these are early warnings of trouble ahead.

It helps to know that this kind of behavior is typical of toddlers, who have conflicting wishes about their push toward autonomy and their anxiety about separating from you. Almost all children go through a "me do it myself" phase, accompanied by temper tantrums and toilet training battles. Handling tantrums, setting limits, and encouraging language development and the expression of feelings consume most of your time and patience.

In the first 2 years, the stages of attachment, the beginnings of separation, and the expression of anger and aggressiveness probably are the same whether your child is adopted or not. Even in homes where the word "adoption" has been used frequently and the child can pronounce it or even say, "I'm Susie, I was adopted from Chicago," the words have little meaning. What is especially important is that your adopted child has the opportunity to pass through the attachment and early separation stages in the same way as a child born to you.

When older babies or children are adopted, their capacity to form relationships may have been disturbed. A series of caretakers and broken attachments through the first months of a child's life can complicate adjustment and compromise the ability to develop trust. You may need to work much harder to let your child know that you care and that you will always be there. Even if your baby received nurturing care before joining your family, s/he can still benefit from your understanding the significance of attachment and the importance of loving interaction.

If you adopt cross-culturally, it will be helpful for you to learn about attachment behavior in that culture. Consider for instance a family who had adopted a 7-month-old Asian baby. When the baby cried, she could not be comforted by holding; she would only quiet down if she were laid on the floor near her mother and spoken to softly. Once she became calmer, she would crawl into her mother's lap for a hug.

There is another example of a baby adopted from Peru who needed to sleep with an

adult for the first few months following adoption. His new crib went unused until he was 15 months old, when his parents were able to help him adjust to sleeping alone. Children who are adopted when they are older usually follow the same attachment and separation paths as other children, but possibly in a different time sequence. This gives you the opportunity to make up for what might have been lost or damaged in earlier relationships.

The first 2 years are crucial to personality development and dramatically influence a child's future. As you grow into your roles as parents, your children also will grow into their place in your family. The next sections provide more information on these techniques.

Ages 2 to 6

If you thought a lot was happening in your child's development in the first 2 years, you will find that the preschool years are filled with activity and nonstop questions. Once children learn to speak, they need only a partner, and the world becomes theirs for the asking and telling. This is when parents begin to feel pressure to explain adoption to their children. It is also when children's ears are wide open to adult conversation and they take in so much more than adults once thought they could. Parents are busy answering as best they can questions such as why the sky is blue, why leaves fall off the trees, why people are different colors, how birds fly, and why a baby brother cannot join the family right now. The more comfortable parents are in trying to answer questions honestly, the more encouraged their children will be to learn. A lack of interest in learning often results from having questions met with too many "I don't knows" or the obvious indifference of parents to their children's curiosity.

Sometimes parents feel so embarrassed about not knowing all the answers to their child's questions or are so afraid of giving the "wrong" answer that they ignore a question or change the subject. In doing so, they often miss a chance to discuss critical feelings with their children. For instance, a little girl visiting a museum with her father asked him why a woman in a painting was crying. She wanted him to pick her up so she could see the painting better, but he felt uncomfortable, took her hand, and moved on. This would have been a good opportunity to discuss why people are sad sometimes and why the little girl thought the woman in the painting was sad.

Children between 2 and 5 years of age have fears, especially about being abandoned, getting lost, or no longer being loved by their parents. They also engage in "magical" thinking and do not distinguish reliably between reality and fantasy. They may be afraid of giants, monsters, witches, or wild animals

Children in this age group become increasingly familiar with separations from loved ones, often because they are attending daycare or preschool programs. They also make new friends outside their family, and their interests broaden. At the same time, they notice that their parents do not know everything and cannot control everything that happens to them. This can be frightening because it threatens their sense of security.

As you observe your children and others, you will notice that both boys and girls imitate their parents' nurturing and care-taking activities. They carry, feed, change, and put to bed their dolls and stuffed animals. They kiss them and sometimes throw them or hit them.

They are mimicking attachment and separation behaviors. If a baby enters the family, many 2-, 3-, and 4-year-olds insist that it is their baby, that they "borned" it or "adopted" it. Sometimes a girl will tell you that it is her baby and that Daddy is the father. A little boy might say that he is going to "marry Mommy when Daddy grows up and dies." If you listen, you will see that your child is trying to make sense of the relationships in the family and to find a way to express the strong emotions of love, hate, and jealousy.

It is puzzling for children to understand why mom and dad get to sleep together while they have to sleep with two trucks and a bunny. You are witnessing what is known as the Electra complex in girls and the Oedipal complex in boys. Little girls may feel jealous of their mothers' grownup relationship with their fathers. They experience a mix of feelings which includes wanting to marry Daddy but feeling competitive and fearful that they will not "measure up." Little boys may want to be mommy's partner in everything and show off their developing "manliness." They do not understand why Daddy should be included but worry that Daddy will be upset with them for the way they feel. All of this behavior is normal for children this age.

There is also an aggressive, competitive side to this stage. You may notice behavior that is challenging, stubborn, and argumentative, usually directed toward the same-sex parent. Girls argue with their mothers about what to wear, what toys to leave at home, and who is the boss of the baby. Boys want to talk about what they will do when they grow up, and even in the most peaceful of families, they will turn all sorts of items into weapons which they yearn to use on the draperies, the baby, and, in frequent moments of frustration and anger, on Daddy.

These behaviors are part of children's working out their awareness of their smallness and insignificance compared to their parents and their urges toward autonomy and independence. They want to be big but also want the benefits of infancy. If they cannot be Mommy or Daddy's partner, they want to be their "lap babies."

Gradually, the intensity of these feelings abates. Children's love for their parents allows them to reconcile the Oedipal or Electra complex by eventually exchanging the wish to marry the parent of the opposite sex for the more realistic desire to grow up to be like the parent of the same sex.

Some version of this scenario occurs in most children, even those raised by a single parent. Sometimes the behavior is expressed directly; other times it is subtle, recognizable only through recalling dreams or in pretend play.

Children who have been traumatized or abused may not show the kind of behavior described here. They may be seductive or fearful, uncertain about the appropriateness of being affectionate, or show symptoms associated with sexual abuse. These children need special help from their parents and

possibly from a skilled therapist before they can feel safe enough to express loving or sexual feelings in their new families. The Child Welfare Information Gateway (Information Gateway) factsheet entitled "Parenting the Sexually Abused Child" is helpful in such cases.

During the preschool years, you may want to respond to your child with humor and tactfully explain that when your child grows up, s/he will find someone just like Mommy or Daddy. Adopted children inevitably wonder to which Mommy and Daddy you are referring. Some researchers believe that this is not the appropriate time to emphasize a child's birth family (Wieder, Schecter). It is difficult enough for children to find their place in the family (as the youngest child, the oldest, etc.) and to come to terms with their gender without having to ponder the meaning of birth parents. It probably is not even possible for a child this age to understand this concept yet.

The Facts of Life: Where Do I Come From? How Did I Get Here?

Most 3- to 6-year-olds do not yet understand the meaning of "being born." If they watch "Sesame Street" or "Mr. Rogers" on television, they may have learned something about how animals are born, and more recently, about how babies are born. They may then start to ask questions about this fascinating subject. Although parents traditionally are nervous about discussing the facts of life with young children, the children usually are curious, unembarrassed, and eager for information. This is a perfect opportunity to introduce the subject of where babies come from, how they get here, and how families are formed. This informa-

tion is a valuable stepping stone in helping your child understand the concept of adoption. It is a time, too, that may awaken painful memories about your own infertility if that was the reason you chose adoption. Discussing birth and the creation of families with your child can be an enriching—and freeing—experience for the whole family.

At this time, adoptive parents must determine what and when they will tell their children about their adoption. Many adoption workers advise parents to introduce the word "adoption" as early as possible so that it becomes a comfortable part of a child's vocabulary and to tell a child, between the ages of 2 and 4 that s/he is adopted. However, some child welfare experts believe that when children are placed for adoption before the age of 2 and are of the same race as the parents, there probably is little to be gained by telling them about their adoption until they are at least 4 or 5 years old. Before that time, they will hear the words but will not understand the concept.

Dr. Steven Nickman, author of the article "Losses in Adoption: The Need for Dialogue," suggests that the ideal time for telling children about their adoption appears to be between the ages of 6 and 8. By the time children are 6 years old, they usually feel established enough in their family not to feel threatened by learning about adoption. Dr. Nickman believes that preschool children still have fears about the loss of their parents and their love and that telling them at that time is too risky. In addition, there is some question about whether a child under 6 years of age can understand the meaning of adoption and be able cognitively to work through the losses

implied by learning that s/he was born into a different family.

Although it is obvious to adults, young children often believe that they are either adopted or born. It is important, when telling them about their adoption, to help them understand that they were born first—and that all children, adopted or not—are conceived and born in the same way. The birth came first, then the adoption.

Waiting until adolescence to reveal a child's adoption to him or her is not recommended. "Disclosure at that time can be devastating to children's self-esteem," says Dr. Nickman, "and to their faith in their parents."

Children Who Are Adopted When They Are Older or Who Are of a Different Race

Children who have been adopted when they are older than 2 or when they are of a different race from their adoptive parents need to be told about their adoption earlier. With older children, who bring with them memories of a past, failure to acknowledge those memories and to have a chance to talk about them can reinforce the attachment problems inherent in shifts in caretakers early in life. In these cases, parents should "work to safeguard the continuity of the child's experience by reminding him or her of his earlier living situation from time to time, still bearing in mind that too frequent reminders might arouse fears of losing his present home," Dr. Nickman suggests.

If your adopted child is of a different race or has very different physical features from your family, you must be cognizant of signs

that s/he is aware of the difference. Your child may have noticed it, or someone else may have commented on it. You will want to explain to your child that the birth process is the same for everyone but acknowledge that people in different cultures have distinguishing physical features and their own rich heritage. Sometimes children who look different from the rest of their family need to be assured that their parents love them and intend to keep them.

For children with developmental disabilities, explanations about birth may be simplified or adjusted to match their ability to comprehend. When children have expressed no interest in the subject, it may be that they are not yet able to benefit from a discussion about it.

In any case, it takes years of periodic returns to the subject of adoption before your children will fully grasp its meaning. Meanwhile, it is most important that you provide an environment that nourishes and encourages learning and the understanding of all important family issues, such as love and aggression, hate and jealousy, sex and marriage, illness and death. At least two studies (Kirk, Hoopes and Stein) suggest that adopted adolescents were better adjusted if they came from families where all emotional issues including adoption were discussed among family members beginning in early childhood.

Children who learn early that it is all right to ask questions and be curious usually carry this behavior over to school and develop a sense of mastery over their lives. That is why both attachment and separation behaviors should be encouraged and endured patiently by parents. Both are necessary for children

to create their identity and to develop and sustain intimate relationships.

Emotional Impact of Adoption

Preschoolers' reactions to adoption are almost entirely affected by the way their parents feel about the adoption and the way they handle it with their children. Children of preschool age will be as excited about the story of their adoptions as other children are by the story of their births. To help make your children feel connected and an important part of the family, share with them the excitement that you felt when you received the telephone call about them, the frantic trip to pick them up, and how thrilled everyone in the family was to meet them. As time goes on and bonds of trust build, your children will be able to make sense of their unique adoption stories.

Elementary School Years

Adoption studies of children in this stage of life are contradictory. While some say that adopted children experience no more psychological problems than nonadopted children (Hoopes and Stein), others find that teachers and parents report more personality and behavior problems and find adopted children to be more dependent, tense, fearful, and hostile (Lindholm and Touliatos, Brodzinsky).

In general, children who have been adopted are well within the normal range academically and emotionally; however, emotional and academic problems may be greater if children were adopted after 9 months of age or if they had multiple placements before being adopted. Since these children are at

greater risk of having attachment problems, their families should consider early intervention and treatment services similar to those available for other adopted children with special needs.

Middle childhood has often been described as a blissful period when children play and visit grandparents, get involved in interesting activities, and have few responsibilities or worries. Nonetheless, as adults we know from our own experiences, that there is a different side to this period between the ages of 6 and 11. The more worrisome serious period is usually experienced in children's inner lives, as indicated by their dreams and fantasies. There their feelings are played out about themselves and their families, their wish to belong outside of the family circle, to have attributes that make others admire them and seek them out, and their contrasting fears that they are dumb, ugly, mean, and useless.

At the same time, their horizons are expanding and they are ready to learn from school, friends, and other adventures outside of their homes. Competitive games and team projects attract them and make them nervous; they search everything and everyone for signs that they are loved and acceptable, while worrying that bad things might happen to pay them back for their seemingly evil deeds and thoughts.

The chief task of elementary school-aged children is to master all of the facts, ideas, and skills that will equip them to progress toward adolescence and independent life. During this time, children are supposed to consolidate their identification with parents and cement their sense of belonging to their family.

It is no wonder that in such a state, even without contemporary pressures resulting from divorce or other family disruptions, that emotional and behavioral problems frequently beset elementary school-aged children. Common problems include hyperactivity, poor school performance, low self-esteem, aggression, defiance, stubbornness, troubled relationships with brothers and sisters, friends, and parents, lack of confidence, fearfulness, sadness, depression, and loneliness. Adoptive parents wonder whether and how much these problems are caused or influenced by adoption or a history of faulty attachment.

Smith and Miroff state in their book, *You're Our Child: The Adoption Experience,* "It is extremely important, and also reassuring, to realize that the most common source of problems are developmental changes which follow a child from infancy to adulthood, not the fact that the child was or was not adopted."

Why Was I Given Away? Loss and Grief in Adoption

Loss is a feeling that runs through the lives of children who have been adopted. It shows itself in different ways at different stages of their lives. But knowing that their birth parents made an adoption plan for them, and then not hearing a lot of information about the birth parents, often makes adopted children feel devalued and affects their self-esteem. Sometimes they feel as though their status in society is ambiguous.

The full emotional impact of that loss comes to children, usually between the ages of 7 and 12, when they are capable of understanding more about the concept of being adopted. It happens because they live more in the world outside of their families and are more tuned in to the world inside their heads. While this is a giant step toward self-reliance, it leaves parents in a quandary about when and how much adoption information to share, and uncertain about whether their child is wanting or dreading to hear it. It is especially difficult at this time to decide what to do or say to children who do not inquire about their birth parents.

Although it may feel awkward, it sometimes helps to think back to your child's life and death questions during the preschool years and introduce the subject yourself. You might preface your conversation with what you would say to an adult. For example, "I just want you to know that if you want to talk about your adoption, I'd be glad to" or "You haven't asked much about it lately, and I thought, now that you're older, you might be thinking about it in a more grownup way." Such an introduction gets across to children that you are interested in talking about the subject and that you are aware of their getting older and more sophisticated in their thinking. In any case, your willingness to "connect" with your children about their adoptions and not to deny the difference between being adopted and being born into a family can help them grieve this important loss.

You can help your children work through their loss if you can be nondefensive about their adoption as well as sensitive to how much they want or need to talk about it at a given time. Do not, however, place undue emphasis on the adoption, as this is likely to make children feel painfully self-conscious about it. But if facts and feelings about adoption are not discussed at all, children's

fantasies about their backgrounds may be acted out unconsciously, thus carrying out their unconscious self-identification as an unworthy person.

Once they have understood the biological facts of life, and something about the social and cultural aspects of family life in their community, children of elementary school age begin to imagine things about their birth parents. One 7-year-old asked if her birth mother looked like their 15-year-old neighbor. An 8-year-old boy asked if his birth father could have been a friend of the family. A 9-year-old reported to her mother that she was looking in the shopping malls for a woman who had a nose like hers.

Although preschoolers want to hear how they were adopted and entered their homes, older children discover the reality that their birth mother relinquished them for adoption and ask why. Just as preschoolers try to make sense of reproduction by developing their own theories and mixing them with what their parents told them, older children try to reconcile their own theories with the available facts. What they learn produces a gamut of emotions ranging from incredulity to sadness, disappointment, anger, and guilt. Children may not express these feelings, but they have to be acknowledged, lived with, and digested before they develop a new understanding of adoption and themselves.

Some researchers think that children must grieve for the loss of the birth parents much in the same way that infertile couples grieve for the loss of a biological baby. Some children feel that they were given up because there was something wrong with them or because they were bad. Some become fearful that they will hurt their adoptive parents'

feelings or make them angry if they want to find out more about their birth parents. Where preschoolers would often be quite open about expressing these feelings, older children have a greater sense of privacy and are not sure that their parents can tolerate their questions or feelings. Older children may, therefore, keep much more to themselves.

A common situation in children of this age, which you may recall from your own elementary school days, is imagining that they had been adopted or kidnapped from another set of parents who were usually better in every way than their own. These parents might have been rich, or even royalty, and they did not make you take vitamins, eat spinach, go to bed at 9 p.m., or refuse to let you watch MTV. When life at home was unpleasant, we could daydream about this "better" family to soothe our angry or sad feelings.

These fantasies provide an outlet for times when children are infuriated or disappointed by their parents, and when they do not know how to cope with their anger toward them. Usually, as a child recognizes that love and hate, anger and affection, can be felt toward people without ruining the relationship completely (i.e., the preschooler's—"I won't be your best friend any more" changes to the 8-year-old's, "I'm so mad at Jenny that I won't sit near her at music today"), these thoughts of another family fade. Then your children can continue to identify with your characteristics, activities, and values.

The fantasy world of the adopted child is complicated by the existence of the birth parents, and is influenced by whatever information is available about them. Some-

times the facts make it more difficult for children to idealize their birth parents or put pressure on them to "choose" to "be just like" or "totally unlike" one or the other set of parents.

Psychological Identification

If your child has had several homes before yours, there is often a brief honeymoon period where s/he will try to be perfect to ensure your love. But soon the sense of loss, hurt, and anger surfaces. Your child may, consciously or not, break your rules, steal, lie, or act out physically or sexually. The child's message is "I'm going to leave here anyway, so I'd better make sure I don't get too close" or "Families don't last, and I'm angry about that."

You will need to help your children build trust and gain confidence that you will not abandon them. Part of that job is helping your children to develop the psychological identification that distinguishes them as individuals.

What is this identification process that is so critical to success and confidence in later life? It takes us back to the initial attachment process, when it is important for babies to make an emotional connection that shape their personalities and make them someone who is a unique individual as well as a member of a particular family.

During the elementary school-age years, children's identity comes from a combination of their genetic heritage, their experience with their families, and what happens to them as they try to find their place in the wider world. They want to be like their peers and their families.

The creation of a family tree, a common elementary school assignment which asks children to construct a portrait of their geographical, ethnic, historical, and birth connections, offers an opportunity and a challenge to the adoptive family. This assignment will bring to the surface knowledge and ignorance about your child's background and legitimize discussion of family facts and secrets.

If there has been openness about adoption and a sensitivity to not insisting on discussing adoption when a child is not receptive, parents will be able to discover from their child what can and cannot be included in the family tree assignment. A 10-year-old, after moving to a new school, said she would like to be the one to decide whether to tell new classmates that she was adopted, because now she was the boss of that information. Is it farfetched to think that a 10-year-old is old enough to be "boss" of her adoptive information? At this age, the child's self-esteem will flourish if she can feel her parents trust her as she learns and masters new facts about herself and the world.

Sometimes during the elementary school years, before or after the family tree experience, children learn about heredity, genes, and "blood relationships." At this time, the adopted child realizes at the highest cognitive and emotional level so far, the differences between biological and adoptive relationships. Reactions to this information are probably as varied as the children and include feelings of relief, a sense of enlightenment, heightened interest in learning more about birth parents, denial of any interest, or feelings of loss and grief.

Remember that all adopted children have feelings about their adoption, and that many times in their development they will struggle with why their birth parents made an adoption plan for them. You can help your children by letting them know that they are not alone in these feelings and that it is all right with you if they express them and try to get explanations for what puzzles or troubles them. The more open family discussions have been from the beginning of verbal communication, the more likely it is that communication will continue no matter how intense or complex the subject becomes.

You may also want to remind yourself and your child that learning about adoption, like learning about life, is an ongoing adventure that you want to share with your child as much as you can, but that you understand that some of this learning has to be pursued alone as well. At this point, your child is old enough to choose the pace at which s/he wants to consider these new ideas. However, you as parents, are still in a position to guide, instruct, and set limits. A 9-year-old who wants, suddenly, to look for her birth mother the day after a fight over bedtime can be told that Mom feels she has to do some maturing before she is ready for that step.

Since these are the years when youngsters appear to seriously confront the "sad side" of relinquishment and adoption, opportunities to meet with and talk to other adoptees their age, as well as with adolescent and adult adoptees, are beneficial. It helps children see a bit into their own futures.

Foreign adoptees can benefit from cross-cultural experiences appropriate to elementary school-aged children. Some children are thrilled to attend an adoption family camp or summer program. Others prefer to process their feelings within their adoptive families or even alone. The more sensitive to your child's feelings you can be, and the more experience you and your child have in discussing feelings together, the more consoling and comforting you can be to each other. You will then survive and eventually triumph over this period of self-discovery and grieving.

Adolescence

No sooner do your children begin to understand the wonders of biology than their own bodies begin the surge of growth toward puberty and the awesome stage of adolescence. Adolescence, for all its newness—it was not considered a distinct stage of life until after the first World War—has quickly acquired a reputation as a difficult and trying period for children and parents. Physical growth changes the person from a child to an adult, in preparation for procreation, but mental and emotional development may take years to catch up with the body. Adolescents' behavior is in transition and not fixed; their feelings about the world and their place in it are tentative and changeable, like a chameleon's.

The adolescent's primary task is to establish a secure sense of identity; the process is arduous, time-consuming, and intense. Establishing a stable identity includes being able to live and work on one's own, to maintain a comfortable position in one's family, and to become a contributing citizen in one's community.

It is the nature of all adolescents, adopted or not, to question everything and everyone. It is also in their parents' nature to worry about their children's futures and their own survival in this period. Almost everyone agrees that, although often extremely difficult, open communication can smooth the process.

Adolescence is a time of trying on and choosing in all aspects of life. Two major aspects of adult identity formation will be choice of work and choice of a partner to love. Teenagers look for and imitate role models. They critically examine their family members (as they did in elementary school), peers, teachers, and all the other heroes and anti-heroes the culture offers from rock musicians and movie stars, to ball players and politicians, to grandparents and peers' older brothers and sisters. They idolize and devalue people, ideas, and religious concepts. They often bond tightly with peers in small groups that are intolerant of all outsiders. They vacillate between criticism of others and harsh self-criticism. They are sometimes supremely self-confident and often in the depths of despair about their abilities and future success.

If normal adolescence involves a crisis in identity, it stands to reason that adopted teenagers will face additional complications because of what some have called "genealogical bewilderment" (Sants). The fact that the adoptee has two sets of parents raises more complicated questions about ancestral history now that intellectual development has assumed adult proportions. The search for possible identification figures may cause the adolescent to fantasize more about birth parents, become interested in specific facts about birth relatives, or wish to search for or meet them.

Although all adopted adolescents have to struggle to integrate their fantasies and future goals with their actual potential and realities, foreign, biracial, and other cross-cultural adoptees (as well as teenagers with physical or emotional disabilities) have additional challenges. They may suffer more from what Erik Erikson calls "identity diffusion," i.e., feelings of aimlessness, fragmentation, or alienation. They may appear outwardly more angry at adoptive parents, and more critical of what their parents did or did not do to help them adjust to their adoptive status. They may withdraw more into themselves, or conversely feel they need to "set off to see the world" in hopes of finding their true identity.

Adolescents often express their reactions to loss by rebelling against parental standards. Knowing that they have a different origin contributes to their need to define themselves autonomously. According to Dr. Nickman, "An adopted son or daughter cannot be expected to be a conformist. If he is, he may be inhibiting an important part of himself for the sake of basic security or out of a sense of guilt or responsibility to his adopters."

It probably helps a child to be told by adoptive parents that they understand their son or daughter's need to take control of his or her own life, and that they stand ready to assist in any way that they can, including giving their blessing to a child who needs "to go it alone" for a while. Of course, a youngster under 17 years of age might be asked to wait until s/he could realistically manage in whatever environment would be encountered.

Searching for Birth Parents

Current adoption practice has mixed opinions about whether, when, how, and with whose help, adoptees should look for more information about or try to initiate a reunion with birth parents. Information on this process is available through Information Gateway. Adoptive parents tend to think about their children's wish to search when they first adopt, and again when confronted with their angry toddlers. The topic resurfaces in adolescence, either raised directly by the child, or when rebellious, defiant behavior such as threats to run away, makes parents wonder if their child is wanting or needing to contact a birth parent. It takes a parent with sturdy self-esteem and more confidence than most of us have to withstand the stony silences and stormy confrontations with teenagers in turmoil.

Parents are often tempted to escape perhaps by abandoning their teenagers who are having toddler-like tantrums, but you and your family will benefit more if you remain calm, stand up for the values you have taught, and continue communication efforts. For some adolescents, searching can be useful, while for many, the urgent activities and decisions of daily life are so pressing that they feel uninterested in or unable to confront such a heavy emotional undertaking. Waiting till they have reached adulthood when their lives will be more settled may be better for the latter group.

Anger, Sex, and Aggression—Again!

Adopted adolescents have the same trouble searching for a comfortable identity as do nonadoptees. Problems involving aggression, sexual activities and pregnancy, delin-quency and substance abuse, social isolation and depression are the most common ones faced by teenagers and their families. Although there appear to be more adoptees percentage-wise in adolescent psychiatric treatment programs than nonadoptees, the majority of these patients tend to be the multiply placed children whose problems stem from a variety of sources, often the least of which is their adoption.

Although sexual identity is an issue for all adolescents, adopted girls have the additional burden of conflicting views of motherhood and sexuality. On one hand there is their perhaps infertile adoptive mother and, on the other, the fertility of their birth mother who did get pregnant and chose not to keep her baby, or possibly had her child taken away from her.

No matter how open communication has been, it is often next to impossible for adolescents to discuss their feelings about sex with their parents. Additionally, the adopted girl, unless she has close friends who are adopted as well, would have difficulty finding an ear understanding and sophisticated enough for this discussion. This may be a time to encourage meeting with other adopted teenagers, either through an organized group or informally, to provide your child with support for some of these sticky issues. Looking for solutions outside of the family is also appropriate for an adolescent for whom one major developmental task is to learn to separate and live independently.

As adolescents move toward greater autonomy, a parent's most difficult task is to create a delicate balance of "to love and let go." Although there are many times when you could encourage your toddler—"me do

it myself"—or elementary school-aged child to "try things alone" or learn a new skill, an adolescent needs to assert his/her independence by establishing differences from you, and real distance. The adolescent needs to take his or her independence or autonomy, rather than be given it.

This often means a period of estrangement, lessened communication, or outright strife. You may want to listen and talk to your friends who have weathered adolescence with their biological children to note the similarities, and as you have tried to do all along, to understand the differences, acknowledge them, and try to work on them with your child.

No matter how much you wanted to be parents, there are many times during the years of child rearing when you might ask, sometimes in humor, and sometimes in sadness, "Why did I ever sign up for this job?" Sometimes you can only reply feebly, "Well, it sure makes life interesting." But finally, you must have faith that the bonding that occurred in the early years between you and your child, the trust that has built as s/he grew up, and the communication that you have established, will come full circle and provide rich and rewarding relationships for you and your adult children.

When You Need Help

In the last 15 years increasing interest and research in child development and parenting has given adoption more attention. Until recently, once a child was placed for adoption by an agency, little else was offered about general child development or rearing;

and if the adoption was a private one, there were no professional helpers. Adoptive parents tried to educate themselves through Dr. Benjamin Spock's 1945 edition of *Baby and Child Care* which offers helpful but brief guidance about adoption.

Now, in addition to Child Welfare Information Gateway, located in Washington, D.C., and the National Adoption Center (NAC) located in Philadelphia, Pennsylvania, there are State and local organizations and programs sponsored by adoption agencies that provide parenting education and other "postadoption" services. Workshops, conferences, and seminars keep parents current with knowledge in the field. There are also support and self-help groups that offer educational and social activities.

The goals of these services are to support and maintain healthy family life, to prevent problems through education, and to make counseling and mental health services available as soon as problems appear. For a list of these agencies, please contact Child Welfare Information Gateway at 703.385.7565 or 1.800.394.3366 or the National Adoption Center at 1.800.TO.ADOPT or 215.735.9988 in Pennsylvania.

How Do You Know You Need Help?

Usually a parent notices that something is wrong, either in the family atmosphere or in a family member. If you have educated yourself about normal child behavior at different ages, chances are you will find yourself questioning behavior in your child that seems out of the ordinary. Sometimes, a teacher, relative, or friend asks if you have noticed a problem. Perhaps your child seems unduly sad or anxious, unable to concen-

trate, is angry or flies off the handle for no obvious reason. You may see behavior that is unusual or not characteristic of your child; sometimes it is the increasing degree of a certain behavior that is troubling.

Perhaps there has been an upsetting event or change, such as a move or loss of job for you or your spouse. Children react to any parental problems that threaten their security. Elementary school-aged children tend to have problems around school; often that is the setting where problems are noticed. Adolescents tend to have identity concerns and authority struggles with their parents or other adults.

All of these possibilities can occur in any family. The adoptive family has the added concern of trying to decide whether or not it is an adoption issue that is troubling the child. If the child is over 6 years of age, it is usually impossible to distinguish adoption from other psychological, social, and educational issues. Treatment must evaluate the child and family and should consider his or her stage of development and the nature of the child's relationship with you (and sometimes with his or her birth parents).

Finding Help

Before seeking professional counseling, use your parenting skills to discover if you can help your child yourself by listening, talking, or making changes in the environment. If you feel your child cannot communicate with you or that your relationship might be part of the problem, it is wise to seek outside assistance.

Because it is so difficult to disentangle adoptive issues from those of normal development, especially once the child has reached elementary school-age, the adoptive family can benefit from professional helpers who have experience working with adoptive families. There are many varieties of therapy, and advantages and disadvantages to each. Sometimes the whole family needs to be involved in therapy. Sometimes your adopted child needs to deal with problems alone.

Ask your agency social worker, a friend with adopted children, your pediatrician, a representative from an adoptive parent support group, your local mental health center, or your local family service agency for recommendations of appropriate helping professionals. You can also contact Information Gateway or NAC for referrals.

This article was written for the National Adoption Information Clearinghouse by Elaine Frank, M.S.W., and edited by Gloria Hochman in 1990.

Bibliography

Books for Parents and Professionals

Brodzinsky, D. and Schechter, M., eds., *The Psychology of Adoption.* (New York: Oxford University Press, 1990).

Dorman, M. and Klein D., *How to Stay Two When Baby Makes Three.* (New York: Ballentine Books, 1985).

Erikson, E.H., *Childhood and Society.* (New York: W.W. Norton and Co., 1986).

Fahlberg, V., "Attachment and Separation" from the series, *Putting the Pieces Together.* (Southfield, MI: Spaulding for Children, 1990).

Fraiberg, S.H., *Magic Years: Understanding and Handling the Problems of Early Childhood.* (New York: Charles Scribner's Sons, 1984).

Hoopes, J.L. and Stein, L.M., *Identity Formation in the Adopted Adolescent, The Delaware Valley Study.* (Washington, DC: Child Welfare League of America, 1985).

Jewett, C.L., *Adopting The Older Child.* (Boston, MA: Harvard Common Press, 1978).

Kirk, D.H., *Shared Fate.* (New York: Free Press, 1964).

Melina, L.R., *Raising Adopted Children: A Manual for Adoptive Parents.* (New York: Harper and Row, 1986).

Parens, H., *Aggression In Our Children: Coping With It Constructively.* (New Jersey: Jason Aronson, Inc. 1987).

Schaeffer, J., and Lindstrom, C., *How To Raise An Adopted Child.* (New York: Copestone Press, 1989).

Smith, J. and Miroff, F., *You're Our Child: The Adoption Experience.* (Lanham, MD: Madison Books, 1987).

Winkler, R.C., Brown, D.W., Von Keppel, M., and Blanchard, A., *Clinical Practice in Adoption.* (New York: Pergamon Press, Inc., 1988).

Articles and Research Reports

Aust, P.H., "Using the Life Story Book in Treatment of Children in Placement." *Child Welfare,* vol. LX no. 8, (September-October 1987) 535-560.

Brodzinsky, D.M., "Adjustment to Adoption: A Psychosocial Perspective" in *Clinical Psychology Review.* Pergamon Journals Ltd., vol. 7 (1987) 25-37.

Cordell, A.S., Nathan, C., and Krymon, V., "Group Counseling for Children Adopted at Older Ages." *Child Welfare,* vol. LXIV no. 2, (March-April 1985) 113-124.

Kopp, C.B. "Risk Factors in Development" in *Infancy and Developmental Psychology,* 4th edition. New York, John Wiley and Sons, (1983) 1081-1088.

Kraft, A.D., Palumbo, J., Mitchell D.L., Woods, P.K., Schmidt, A.W., and Tucker, N.G., "Some Theoretical Considerations on Confidential Adoptions: Part III: The Adopted Child" in *Child and Adolescence Social Work Journal,* vol. 2, (1985) 139-153.

Lindholm, B.W. and Touliatos, J. "Psychological Adjustment of Adopted and Nonadopted Children." *Psychological Reports,* vol. 46, (1980) 307-310.

Nickman, S.L. "Losses in Adoption: The Need for Dialogue." *The Psychoanalytic Study of the Child,* vol. 40, (1985) 365-397.

Sants, H.J. "Genealogical Bewilderment in Children With Substitute Parents." *British Journal of Medical Psychology,* vol. 37, (1964) 133-141.

Schecter, M.D., Carlson, P.V., Simmons, J.Q., III, and Work, H.H., "Emotional Problems in the Adoptee." *Archives of General Psychiatry,* vol. 10, (1964) 109-118.

Wieder, H. "On Being Told of Adoption." *Psychoanalytic Quarterly,* (1977) 1-22.